BYGONE SURREY

BYGONE SURREY

EDITED BY

GEORGE CLINCH

AND

S. W. KERSHAW, M.A.,F.S.A.

Republished by S.R. Publishers Ltd., 1970
Originally published London, 1895

© 1970 S.R. Publishers Limited,
East Ardsley, Wakefield,
Yorkshire, England.

ISBN 0 85409 617 5

Reprinted in England by Scolar Press Ltd.
Menston, Yorkshire, U.K.

BYGONE SURREY.

NONSUCH PALACE.

(From an old engraving.)

BYGONE SURREY.

EDITED BY

GEORGE CLINCH

AND

S. W. KERSHAW, M.A., F.S.A.

LONDON :
SIMPKIN, MARSHALL, HAMILTON, KENT, & CO., LTD.

HULL :
WILLIAM ANDREWS & CO., THE HULL PRESS.

1895.

Preface.

IN issuing "Bygone Surrey" it is felt that an apology is due for the unusually long space of time which has elapsed between the first announcement of the book and the appearance of the finished volume. The delay has arisen from a variety of causes, into which it is needless to enter; the editors, however, wish to explain that they are not in any way responsible for it.

From the first the editors have received many acts of kind assistance and suggestions, for which they now desire to express their sincerest appreciation. The contributors, by their special and local antiquarian knowledge, have long been identified with the county, and thanks are particularly due to them for their various papers contained in this volume. Thanks are also due to Messrs. W. Blackwood and Sons for permission to use some of the engravings which illustrate

Mr. Cave-Browne's valuable article on " Lambeth Palace."

A melancholy interest attaches to the graceful article on " Wanborough," contributed by the late Lady West, which the authoress corrected for the press only a few days before her death.

September, 1894.

Contents.

BYGONE SURREY.

Historic Surrey.

BY GEORGE CLINCH.

IN attempting to take a rapid survey of the history of any locality we run a great danger of forgetting those earlier chapters of its book of history which are written upon the stones and rocks at our feet, and for the tracing out of which we have neither documentary nor traditional guidance. We have no intention of prefixing to this necessarily inadequate account of Bygone Surrey any attempt at a geological review, but probably no one can fail to see how great an influence must have been exerted by Surrey's physical form and mineral products upon the life of man, " who comes, and tills the field, and lies beneath."

Who that has felt the fresh breezes blow from the crest of the North Downs, and, looking below, has seen the smiling, undulating country

1

stretching out before him away to the greyish-purple crests of the South Downs with their famous Devil's Dyke, Cissbury, and Chanctonbury heights,—who that has watched the rain-clouds burst against the noble crests of Leith Hill, and other ancient landmarks, can doubt that the same feelings of awe, of tenderness, and of affection, which we feel for this delightful county, must have been felt, to some extent at least, by our earliest forefathers? Who can doubt that the eternal hills, which seem as if protecting the quiet Surrey villages nestled beneath them, must have inspired in the mediæval mind sentiments of peace and contentment? Surely the o'er-shadowing brow of weather-beaten chalk-down must have had some lesson of consolation and companionship for the very earliest inhabitants of this district; as well as for the pious visitants to Becket's shrine, who, by paths which were of hoary antiquity even in their day, wended their way under cover of this natural rampart.

It has been asserted that every important building which dominates a large area of country has a certain, and often unsuspected, influence upon the minds of those who dwell around it and daily behold it in the course of the ordinary

business of life. If this be true of buildings—
the work of man—how much greater must be the
influence of the glorious prospects which are
spread out ever before the eyes of the shepherds
and peasants of the weald and downs of Surrey!

There is small reason to wonder at the fine
patriotic spirit which, like a flame, has blazed
forth on the appearance of the warning beacon
in times of public danger and of national
rejoicing. The coming of the great Armada
was flashed forth by signal-fires from Surrey's
hill-tops ;

" And eastward straight from wild Blackheath the warlike
  errand went,
And roused in many an ancient hall the gallant squires
  of Kent.
Southward from Surrey's pleasant hills flew those bright
  couriers forth ;
High on bleak Hampstead's swarthy moor they started
  for the north ;
And on, and on, without a pause, untired they bounded
  still :
All night from tower to tower they sprang, they sprang
  from hill to hill."

At the time, too, when Victoria's jubilee was
celebrated throughout the land, the fires of Leith
Hill again blazed forth in token of rejoicing.

Our forefathers early discovered the value of

these hill-tops for strategic purposes, and a good
many of the highest points to this day bear
evidences of fortification in the form of earth-
works, more or less extensive and well-preserved.
Surrey possesses many evidences of military
works of very early date, and the hoary walls
of the castles of Guildford and Farnham speak
eloquently of the defensive structures which were
built during mediæval times.

One of the chief features of commercial
importance, however, is to be found in the roads,
which in Roman, and even earlier times, traversed
the area which is now Surrey. The Pilgrims'
Way, which is probably a thoroughfare of extreme
antiquity, and other roads which provided means
of communication between the sea-coast and the
interior of the country, are more particularly
treated in another chapter, but, generally speaking,
they may be said to be a very important institution and a clear indication of Surrey's early
commercial development. Along these roads
travelled military as well as commercial operations.

Everyone who is in the slightest degree
acquainted with the interior and less populated
parts of Surrey, must have been struck with the
remarkably picturesque homesteads and cottages

scattered all over the county. Many of these dwellings are of considerable antiquity, and they doubtless owe their appearance of welcome and comfort, in a large degree, to their warmth of tone, as well as to those features so pleasantly suggestive of shelter—a large roof with ample eaves, and the other indications of protection and stability.

Although no very important events in our national history have taken place here, Surrey has often been the scene of civil and political strife. In the days of King John, the discontented and insurgent barons frequently held councils at Reigate; and, in the time of the civil wars between Charles I. and his parliament, Kingston was repeatedly visited by both armies, and was the scene of occasional skirmishes. The chief part of Surrey's story, however, is of a pacific nature. Her sons and daughters have comprised some of the foremost names in the fields of letters, arts, sciences, and the peaceful occupations of agriculture and the industrial arts.

A Glance at Primitive Surrey.

By FRANK LASHAM.

THE earliest type of men, known to science
as Palæolithic (or old stone) of the river
drift period, have been found to have existed
in the neighbourhood of Farnham : hitherto
this early type of men have been only known
in the portion of Surrey comprised in the
Thames valley, but, in 1887, after prolonged
search, Palæolithic haches, or celts, were found
in situ in the high level beds of river gravels
or drift, which occur about 364 feet above the
mean sea level, and are 150 feet above the level
of the present River Wey. These beds appear
to be of great age, they lie superimposed upon
beds of greensand, and present all the usual
characteristics of drift gravels ; a few mammalian
remains have been found, but they are not
plentiful ; upwards of 500 implements, many
of them very large and beautifully worked, have
been collected from these beds. Some of the
haches appear just as left by their ancient makers,

whilst others are very ochreous, rolled, and
abraded, showing how great must have been the
changes wrought in the aspect of the country
since the day when they were first made. The
abraded specimens are generally found at the
lower levels. Collections of these implements
have been made by Mr. H. A. Mangles, of
Seale, and myself. Mammalian remains were
discovered in cutting the new railway at
Guildford, but nothing was then discovered that
had reference to the "genus homo." The
gravels of the Tillingbourne have also yielded
similar remains, but no implements. A few
isolated Palæoliths have been found at Tilford,
Peperharrow, Frimley (Blackwater Gravels), and
near Farley Heath (lacustrine), Albury, and
Tilford. A paper on Palæolithic Man in West
Surrey is printed in the *Surrey Archæological
Collections* (Vol xi., Part I., pp. 25-29).

The descendants of these men have left many
traces of their existence in the whitened celts
and other shaped flints, representing the early
Neolithic (or new stone) age, which lie scattered
over the ridges of the Hog's Back and along the
chalk hills in many districts of Surrey. In the
museum at the Charterhouse, Godalming, there

is a collection made from a wide area around
Puttenham.   It is very probable that the
county of Surrey in these early days was densely
wooded and difficult of access, but there would
seem to have been a large Neolithic population,
" flakes " of flint, one of the principal evidences of
man's handiwork, being easily found on the
surface of very many fields.   These Neolithic folk
were more civilized than their predecessors,
and it is generally understood that our present
race sprang from them.   The latest Neolithic
stage is represented by the finely polished celts
of flint, arrowheads, scrapers, etc., which are
somewhat plentiful.   At Wanborough, on the
Hog's Back, evidences of the presence of these
folk, as also of those of the next, or bronze
epoch, and of the Romans and Saxons, have been
traced.   This indicates a district of great interest
to the antiquary.   Stone implements have also
been found at or near Guildford, Tilford, Frensham, St. Martha's, Crooksbury, The Chantries,
Godalming, Seale, and other localities.   Blackheath, a wild spot near Albury, now probably as
it was in the Neolithic days, has yielded a large
number of flakes, which are bleached of a
peculiar whiteness.   At Ash, near Farnham, a

very fine polished flint celt was discovered, and others have been found at Wisley. Of the Bronze Age not many implements have been found. Wanborough, Farley Heath (Romano-British Camp), Guildford, Crooksbury (near Farnham), Godalming, Bagshot, etc., have yielded specimens. The Thames valley has, however, a good reputation with regard to discoveries of bronze weapons and implements. Camps and tumuli exist, but not in any great numbers. Tumuli (opened) are to be seen at Frensham, Woking, the Hog's Back, and Puttenham.

General Pitt Rivers opened two tumuli on Whitmoor Common, near Guildford, and found cremated interments and urns. Romano-British camps exist at Anstiebury (Dorking), Hascombe, Puttenham, Farley Heath (Albury), and Aldershot.

Lambeth Palace.

By Rev. J. Cave-Browne, m.a.

THERE are few buildings now left in London, or even through the length and breadth of England, which are so full of history, so instinct with the life of bygone ages, as Lambeth Palace. Its river front tells its tale of Plantagenet, and Tudor, and Stuart dynasties. It tells of the keen struggle between the monks of Christchurch, Canterbury, and their would-be independent Primate, Baldwin, the Crusader, and Hubert Walter; of the imperious Savoyard, Boniface; of the munificent Chichele; of the proud and powerful Cardinal Morton; of the ill-advised and ill-fated Laud; of the saintly Juxon. It is alive with memories of feuds between Primate and Pontiff; between the Crown and the Church; and lastly between the Prelacy and the Parliament—but never with the people—each and all have left their impress and their record on the walls of this goodly, though sombre, pile of buildings.

Time was, as its very name indicates, when Lambeth was a "loam-hythe," or muddy harbour, a low swampy marsh ; probably the upper outlet of Canute's canal. Even so late as Elizabeth's reign the adjacent ground, now a network of streets teeming with a busy population, was but a sporting ground, rich in waterfowl and other game, and indeed within the memory of middle-aged manhood, retaining the name of "The Marsh," and in the centre of the present Westminster Bridge Road, the historic Marsh-Gate.

But to return to the Palace itself, and to the circumstances under which it became the official residence of the "Primate of all England." This seemingly undesirable site originally belonged to the Crown, and was granted by the Confessor to his sister, Goda, and by her to the See of Rochester. A property so remote and so unproductive was of comparatively little value to them ; so when Archbishop Baldwin proposed to Gilbert de Granville, then Bishop of Rochester, to exchange it for a range of rich pasture land near Darente, belonging to the See of Canterbury, the exchange was effected, subject to the condition of a yearly supply of fish, especially lampreys, from the Thames, for the monks of St. Andrew's at Rochester, even though the Medway flowed close under their own walls.

But a site which was held of so little value by the Rochester chapter, possessed no ordinary attractions for Archbishop Baldwin. It would bring him into closer contact with the Court, which had now permanently removed from Winchester to Westminster, and with the King, with whom he stood in high favour, as already " Chief Justitiary " (or Chief Justice), and expectant Chancellor. Nor was it only, or primarily, as a residence that the Archbishop desired it ; his quarrel with his monks, and his endeavour to establish an independent Chapter of secular canons, who should act as his advisers, and not as his constant opponents, had made him resolve to find some suitable locality for placing them away from the Metropolitical city ; and having failed to carry out his plan, first at St. Stephen's Hackington, and then at Maidstone, he hoped to be more successful in the more distant corner of Lambeth. But even here the animosity of his monks, and their influence at Rome, thwarted him ; and filled with the Crusading zeal which Richard, who had now come to the throne, inspired, he went to the Holy Land, to die there, —his Lambeth scheme a failure.

Hubert Walter, who after the short interval of five years, during which the sickly Reginald de Josceline filled the See, succeeded his chivalrous friend and patron Baldwin, at once resolved to carry out his design of the Chapter at

LAMBETH PALACE—GARDEN VIEW, PRIOR TO 1829.

Lambeth: but again the influence of the monks at Rome defeated his object. The foundation of the Chapel, and probably of the adjacent tower, was laid, and the walls were beginning to rise, when a summary mandate for their demolition arrived, and the monks had the satisfaction of seeing the progress of the work stopped, never again to be resumed in its original design. Lambeth was not to have a Chapter ; but out of that forbidden design was to rise some years after, under circumstances to be described, what was to prove the historic home of so many distinguished successors of a Baldwin and a Hubert Walter.

Now, anyone wishing to trace the successive steps by which this massive pile rose to its present noble proportions, must place himself in the shrubbery, under the north side of the Chapel. There, in the lower portion of that wall, he will see what, in all probability, remains of the earliest work of Hubert Walter, if not of Baldwin himself. The eye of the expert will detect masonry there which belongs to the twelfth century, rising two or three feet above the ground ; above this a change in the work marks the hand of the mason of the next century, which carries the mind on to the next effort to carry on the design. This was probably due to Stephen Langton, who is credited with having added some portion of the building. His may have been the commencement of that Tower, of which the projecting buttress or turret, containing the spiral stair, alone remains, leading up to the rooms in the Water Tower, and having, at its extreme top, the room wrongly called "the Lollards' Prison," of which mention will be made presently.

The next stage in the rise of the building is far more important and clearly defined, that which is connected with the name of Archbishop Boniface, the truculent Savoyard, whose ruthless attack on the monks of St. Bartholomew, in Smithfield, brought down upon him the peremptory mandate from Pope Urban IV. to repair, or build anew, the "*edificia*" at Lambeth, which had fallen into great disrepair. In the lovely lancet windows of the Chapel may be seen his share of the work, closely corresponding, as they do, in date as well as character, with those in the nave of the Temple Church. The Chapel was clearly a superstructure on the earlier Crypt, which, like the lower portion of the outer wall already noticed, formed the foundation of the building which Archbishops Baldwin or Hubert Walter had designed, but were never permitted to complete. Ducarel thinks that not only the Chapel, but also the foundations of the Great Hall, formed part of the expiatory work of Boniface.

The west door of the Chapel, with its deep,

bold hood-moulding, would suggest that his building did not extend further westward; but that that portion, of which only the Turret stair now remains, was the addition of Stephen Langton. And that when, in the middle of the fifteenth century, Chichele added his noble Tower, he cleared away all the rest of the then existing building, retaining the massive Turret staircase, as being the only means of access to the upper rooms of his Tower.

At the top of this Turret, with its small square window and projecting fireplace, is what is commonly called the " Lollards' Prison." Its massive double doors, with weighty chain and hasps, no doubt proclaim it to have been designed for a place of confinement; but the names and figures on the oak panelling point rather to the middle of the seventeenth than to the fifteenth century; and there is, too, sad historical evidence that it was so used for the Loyalist prisoners under Cromwell, while, as will be more fully shown in speaking of the adjoining Tower, there is none that any Lollard was ever confined here.

The history of the adjoining Tower demands fuller notice. It was undoubtedly built by that munificent Primate, Chichele. The " Stewards'

Accounts" (*Compotus Ballivorum*), still preserved in the Muniment Room, giving every detail of the cost, show that, between 1424 and 1441, he expended on it £278, a sum equivalent to £5,000 of our currency ; and, on a shield at the base of the little niche which remains between the windows of the second story on the river face, were his arms impaling those of the See, under the figure of Thomas a Becket.

Archbishop Chichele appears in the history of the English Church under two very different characters, whether he be regarded from the Romish or the Anglican point of view ; as the munificent founder of All Souls' College, Oxford, or as the reputed persecutor of the Lollards. Now by a singular coincidence

NICHE ON THE WALL OF THE WATER TOWER, LAMBETH PALACE.

Lambeth represents him in both characters, as the real benefactor by adding this conspicuous Tower to adorn this pile of buildings ; and also as the supposed scourge of the Lollards, for whose special persecution he was in subsequent ages said to have built it—a charge which has, ever since the Revolution, become a stereotyped idea, and is too often still perpetuated by giving to this Tower the name of " The Lollards' Tower."　Now it is impossible to read the life of Archbishop Chichele without seeing that, while he was not without the then dominant conception of religious duty in supporting what he believed to be the " True Faith," even to the extent of prosecuting in the Ecclesiastical Courts those who were deemed to be guilty of heresy, a spirit of persecution, even for the truth's sake, was wholly foreign to his beneficent nature.　Many an act of severity against the Lollards, or Wickliffites, during his Primacy, and performed in his name, was but the reluctant obedience of peremptory orders from Rome.　Burdened, as he was, with the legacy of Arundel's cruel enactments, especially that Papal Bull " De Heretico Comburendo," and with Cardinal Beaufort's overpowering influence at York, Chichele was scarcely a free agent. Many of his acts were under compulsion ; under threat of Papal censure.　His true character, such as was seen in his private life, has been well described by his own University, " that he stood in the sanctuary of God as a firm wall that heresy could not shake, nor simony undermine, he was the darling of the people, and the fosterparent of the clergy." Was this a man likely to turn what he designed as his own residence into a prison-house for heretics ? he, too, who had obtained the passing of what is known as " The Whipping Act," an Act by which he doubtless saved many a life at the expence of a flogging ? Be it remembered, also, that the one room which was undoubtedly used as a prison, was not in the Tower he built, but at the top of that Turret stair, which, as we have seen, belonged to that earlier building. Nor was the Tower ever associated with the name of Lollards for at least three hundred years. Not an allusion to a Lollard having having been imprisoned here occurs in the voluminous records of old John Foxe, or any contemporary writer. When the Fire of London had swept away Old St. Paul's and its surroundings, and among them the real " Lollards' Prison," associated with the persecutions of Bonner and his colleagues, and the only seemingly appropriate place for such a tradition could be found in the suggestive old room at the top of the Turret stair, it was easy to transfer the scene from St. Paul's to Lambeth, and there it still clings with sad pertinacity. And there it probably will cling in spite of the refutation of history.

Among the many calumnies with which the fair fame of this Primate has been assailed, is one which the main room of this Tower suggested. In its centre stands a stout post, with which, supported no doubt by Chichele's "Whipping Act," local tradition for many years represented as the scene of many a Lollard whipping. A calumny as baseless as the others; for that post was evidently an insertion of the 18th century for the purpose of supporting the heavy beam which spans the room.

Within the last half century there remained in the north wall of this room a memorial of a now lost feature of this tower, and the one which accounted for the name by which it was rightly known for centuries, as Chichele's "Water-Tower." In that wall was a doorway, the *raison d'être* of which was disclosed by the corresponding marks on the outer wall. Here may still be traced the outline of a doorway, and also of a flight of stone steps which led down to the river, for in those days the Thames flowed up a narrow inlet to the very walls of the Palace.

Down those steps did successive Archbishops

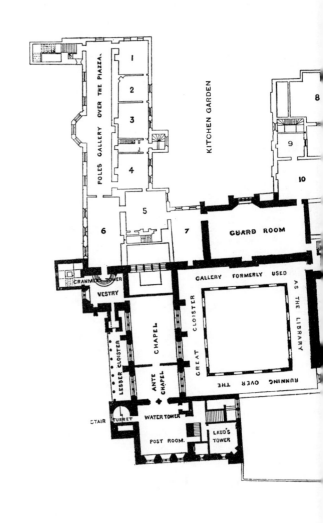

LAMBETH PALACE.

SHEWING THE OLD ARRANGEMENT BEFORE
1829.

1. Bed Room.
2. ,, ,,
3. ,, ,,
4. Library.
5. Waiting Room.
6. Dining Room.
7. Waiting Room.
8. Kitchen.
9. Bed Room.
10. Drawing Room.

Scale of Feet.

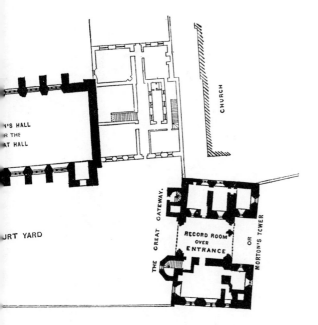

daily pass to their barge, moored at the foot, and "took water" on old Thames highway, or crossed over to Westminster. It was down these steps that the body of Archbishop Deane, in 1503, was borne on its way to burial at Canterbury. Here, too, passed Anne Boleyn after hearing her doom at the mouth of Cranmer in the Crypt : here, too, passed the good Bishop Fisher, and his fellow prisoner, the wise Sir Thomas More, to the Tower, after the Commission which sat in the Great Hall; and probably at these stairs occurred the memorable interview between Cranmer and Henry, when the King warned him of the plot laid against him by the Canterbury magnates. Now, under the repairs carried out a few years since by the Ecclesiastical Commissioners, all trace of this historic feature of the " Water Tower " has disappeared : the inner door and its framework, which the writer has often seen, was cleared out by some ignorant contractor.

Every portion of this Tower proclaims it as having been designed as an official and private residence. The Post-room, with its wide-spanned oaken roof and rich ornamental carvings at every junction of the ribs which panel it off, formed a fitting audience chamber, while the upper stories contained spacious private and sleeping apartments, and are now utilised by several Bishops during their attendance in Parliament.

In one of the upper rooms is an opening in the floor, to which also local tradition has attached an awful meaning. It used to be suggested by former showmen of the Palace, Was it not for the purpose of throwing down into the river below the bodies of poor Lollards, perhaps sometimes alive, that so they might be put out of sight, and out of remembrance? No. Its object, running through the several storeys, was for a far more ordinary use. It was "Guard-robe" not an "Oubliette."

After this full account of the Water Tower, it is time to pass on to the smaller Tower attached to it on the south side. This was added by Archbishop Laud. Finding, as we have seen, no other means of access to the upper rooms of the main tower, he added this for the sake of a staircase, and to obtain a few additional rooms, for chaplains and visitors. For the Tower which Cranmer had built at the east end of the Chapel, was only for his own use, and contained no accommodation for any of his dependants or

friends. By means of the new staircase, easy
access was gained to the rooms in the earlier
Tower.

We now turn to the Tower at the entrance
gate. The casual passer-by along the Thames
embankment, as he approaches Lambeth Palace,
may be forgiven if he sees in that sombre pile,
that gloomy brick gateway, something suggestive of a prison. Yet was it once the dwelling
of one of the most powerful of the Archbishops
of Canterbury, Lord Cardinal Morton, erected
by him for his own use. In the square block on
the left, the second storey, which was reached by
a spiral stone stair through a low door on the
north face of the building, was his range of
private apartments, his sitting room, and in it, in
a recess in the wall, now used as a cupboard, his
folding camp bed, screened out of sight during
the day by closed doors. The entire space of the
central block formed his "State Apartment," his
Reception room, or as we might say, his
"Audience Chamber," with its floor rush-strewn,
and its walls lined with plaited reeds. Such was
the height of social and state luxury, when
Cardinal Morton raised that Tower about four
hundred years ago. On the ground floor, on the

left hand under the gateway, were the official
apartments of the See, the Registry of Pre-
rogative Court, etc., now used as the Porter's
kitchen, while the right hand block of the
Tower presented another aspect of life of those
days : here was the Warder's room, and leading
out of it an inner room, now a scullery, which
then served the purpose of a place of confinement,
or prison, as the massive iron rings in the wall
still testify, for the reception of any heretical
or criminous clerks of a violent or dangerous
character, while the more peaceful and orderly of
such victims of suspicion enjoyed the greater
freedom of the upper portion of this Tower,
having access to it by a spiral stair behind the
warder's room ; from which, however, an iron
grating, opening on to the stair itself, enabled the
Argus-eyed watchman within to see each *detenu*,
as he passed up or down. Such is the gateway
known as Morton's Tower, built in 1480.

Passing through the inner arch of this
gateway, the first object that attracts the eye
is the imposing building on the right hand
commonly known as "Juxon's Hall," and now
used as the Public Library. Though at present
betraying signs of the Renaissance period, its

history carries back the mind to a far more remote time. No less weighty an authority than Ducarel suggests that it probably formed a part of the original design of Hubert Walter, or even Baldwin, for a spacious hall formed an essential part of the entourage of every baronial or episcopal residence in days when hospitality and charity were wont to hold so prominent a place in the daily life of the dignitaries in the State or the Church.

Whatever may have been the exact date of its original foundation, it clearly existed as early as the beginning of the fourteenth century, being mentioned as the "Aula Magna" in the "*Compotus Ballivorum,*" or "Stewards' Accounts," in the days of Archbishop Reynolds, and was a few years after repaired, if not rebuilt, by Archbishop Chichele at the time when he was rearing the "Water Tower." Then, two centuries later, Archbishop Parker "covered the Great Hall with shingles." But the year 1648, a year so fatal to all belonging to the Church as well as to the Crown, saw the whole building, having been assigned to the Royal Regicide, Colonel Scott, razed to the ground, and the rich time-honoured materials put up to sale !

One of the many noble works of restoration
undertaken by the liberal Archbishop Juxon, was
the rebuilding of this Hall, at a cost of above
£10,000, representing a sum well-nigh ten times
its amount at the present day. So earnest was
his desire to make this as nearly as might be a
" restoration " rising on the old lines, and retaining
as closely as he could its old character, that, as an
historian of Surrey says, " Not all the persuasions
of men versed in literature, and of his friends,
could induce him to rebuild it in the modern way,
though it would have cost less money." And to
protect it against the modernising taste which
then prevailed, he made this provision in his
will :—" If I happen to die before the Hall at
Lambeth be finished, my executor to be at the
charge of finishing it, according to the model
made of it, if my successor give leave." It would
seem as if the restored building was not permitted to altogether escape the prevailing fancy
of the day, for the balls crowning the buttresses
outside instead of the finials of the earlier
building, and those on the inside replacing
the carved pendant of an earlier roof,
betray the hand of the Renaissance designer.
As does the Louvre rising from the centre,

LAMBETH PALACE—THE GREAT HALL (NOW THE LIBRARY).

and bearing on its vane the arms of Archbishop
Juxon.

This Hall is ninety-three feet long and thirty-
eight broad, rising at the pitch of the roof to
an elevation of above fifty feet.   The roof itself,
with its massive oaken hammer-beams and
pendant-posts, resembling those of Westminster
Hall, and also what remains of the Royal Palace
at Eltham, carries back the mind to the grand
and graceful architecture of the fourteenth rather
than that of the seventeenth century.   Nor
have we to go back a hundred years for evidences
of that earlier life.   Within the present century
there stood along the side walls the old tables
at which the lavish hospitality of feudal times
was wont to be dispensed; where Robert
Winchelsea, after feasting his friends and
retainers, distributed the remains of the banquet
among the poor who thronged to his gate,
thus establishing the well-known "Lambeth
Dole."   Here, too, besides such more ordinary
banquets, were held the "Consecration Banquets,"
at which each newly-consecrated Prelate of the
Province of Canterbury held high feast among his
brother bishops, a custom which only ceased
half a century ago.

This Hall, too, has often been the witness of very different scenes. Convocation has more than once sat here. Councils, too, of the English Church, in the days of Boniface, and Peckham, and Simon de Meopham; and be it remembered, in later years, in the more far-reaching form of a " Pan-Anglican Synod" under Archbishops Longley, and Tait, and Benson.

But perhaps the most startling events with which this Hall is connected, are some of the Special Commissions which have sat in it. It was here that Cranmer extorted from the clergy the oath which transferred the Supremacy of the Church from the Pope to the King, in 1534. Among them stood the aged, saintly Fisher, Bishop of Rochester, who had been confessor and trusted councillor to the King's illustrious grandmother, " the Lady Margaret," Countess of Beaufort; and by his side " the noblest layman England ever had," so history has pronounced him, Sir Thomas More, the learned and true: both falling victims to Henry's tyrannical autocracy.

Such trials have of late years given place to far more peaceful scenes, when Churchmen, lay and clerical, so often meet here to discuss subjects ecclesiastical and philanthropic, or, if needs be, for judicial litigation.

But it is under its present aspect that the Great Hall is best known as the "Lambeth Library," in which it has associated with it the names of some of the luminaries of their day. It seems strange that, considering the profound learning of so many of the preceding Primates, there should have been no Public Library attached to the Palace till a comparatively recent period. To Bancroft, in the days of Queen Elizabeth, it is indebted for the first contribution of a private library to the See. Even his bequest had a narrow escape from being otherwise appropriated or scattered to the winds under the ruthless hands of the Parliamentarian spoilers in 1646, but it was a staunch Cromwellian (so to say), no other than John Selden, who rescued and restored it to Lambeth, where it has remained to form the nucleus of the present Library. Other Primates had accumulated goodly stores of literary wealth, but had bequeathed them to different colleges : Parker to Corpus Christi, Cambridge; Laud divided his between his own college, St. John's, Oxford, and the Bodleian Library; Sancroft his to Emanuel College, Cambridge; while that of Wake passed, with his magnificent collection of coins, to Christ Church, Oxford. Thus did the Lambeth Library, as Evelyn has happily put it, ebb and flow like the Thames, that run beside it, with every Prelate.

Still the wealth and treasures of the permanent library remain undiminished, when we think of the Registers of the Southern Province, almost without interruption, from the time of Peckham ; its Miscellaneous MSS. too : its rare collection of printed books prior to 1600, the Parliamentary Survey of Church lands during the Commonwealth : the later " Notitiæ Parochiales : " the Biblical MSS. bequeathed by Archbishop Tenison, and its illuminated Missals, etc., it may truly claim high rank among the libraries of the world.

Some of its librarians also have reflected the lustre of its literary wealth : Henry Wharton, Edmund Gibson, Andrew Coltee Ducarel, Henry John Todd, Samuel Roffey Maitland, and William Stubbs, the present learned Bishop of Oxford, among them.

In a large bay window on the west side of the upper end of the Hall, are collected together

several rare and valuable specimens of stained
glass, chiefly heraldic, rescued from the old
galleries and corridors, which were removed
when Archbishop Howley, under the able designs
of Mr. Blore, erected the present imposing range
of domestic apartments.

Opposite this window, is a handsome doorway
of Italian character, introduced by Archbishop
Juxon, opening into a spacious lobby in which a
staircase leads to what is one of the most
interesting and historic portions of this ancient
pile.

It was commonly known as the "Guard-
Chamber," for such was its original use, carrying
back the mind to the days when Primates were
feudal Lords, with armed retinues. Lying
between the public Banquetting Hall and the
private portion of the Palace, it tells of times
when spiritual lords might require the protection
of temporal weapons. The battle axes and lances
which down to the days of Laud might be seen
standing beside the empty coats of mail, long
after the living men-at-arms had disappeared
from the scene, have given place to a goodly
array of portraits of successive primates from that
period, and a few of even earlier date. And

while the line of Primates appears in unbroken succession from Laud to Benson, so also is the continuity of art illustrated on the walls of this old Guard Chamber. Here are originals of Holbein and Vandyke, each with its own history, of Kneller and Hogarth, of Sir Joshua Reynolds and Romney, Sir Thomas Lawrence, Sir Martin Shee, of Richmond, and Herkomer. While in the gallery alongside, as also in the private rooms, are portraits of the leading contemporaries of these occupants of the See of Canterbury, giving a still wider historical interest to the official home of the " Primates of all England."

Running eastward from the group of Towers, already described, stands the exquisite chapel, which perhaps more than any other part of this historic range of buildings, is rich in the associations of the past; containing as it does mementoes of the successive Primates over a period of above 800 years, from the days of the ruthless Savoyard Boniface, to those of the peaceloving statesman Archibald Campbell Tait, and the artloving and learned Edward White Benson.

The western doorway, opening from the " Postroom " in the Water Tower, with its bold deep hood moulding, shows that it was originally exposed to the open air, and standing on a raised terrace, formed the main entrance to the Chapel. Its construction is noteworthy. A semicircular arch encloses two single-cusped arches, the outer jambs consisting of four graceful columns, with their capitals, as also their bases, composed of solid blocks of purbeck marble laid horizontally, forming a strikingly bold and yet elegant device.

The chapel itself is seventy-two feet long and twenty-five broad, divided into four bays of triplet lancets on either side, the first bay is partitioned off by a screen, and forms an atrium or ante-chapel. The east window consists of five graduated lancets, each, like the other windows of the chapel, having light shafts of Purbeck marble.

Under the chapel is a crypt of the same size, and of much earlier date, being no doubt part of the original building of Baldwin or Hubert Walter, as is evident from the bold groining of the roof, and the character of the capitals of the piers which support it. This was no doubt of a much higher pitch; but the frequent filling in of the floor to raise it above the level of the river, which was constantly flooding it, has in time reduced it. In its earlier state it doubtless was

used for judicial rather than for religious purposes; and as such must have witnessed some
stirring events. Here it was no doubt that that
imperious Primate Boniface, in the year 1249,
fulminated his ecclesiastical thunders against the
Prior and Monks of St. Bartholomew the Great,
in Smithfield, and the gentle-born and learned
Fulco Basset, Bishop of London. Here, too,
probably was enacted that scene in the year 1378,
when the brave John Wickliffe stood before
Archbishop Sudbury, arraigned for heretical
teaching, and the rescue came, not as it had done
at St. Paul's, by the commanding presence of
John of Gaunt, but by the rush of Lollard
citizens who bore him off in safety. Here again
in 1536 the unfortunate Anne Boleyn heard
Cranmer pronounce the dread sentence which
was to consign her back to the Tower and to the
block.

Upon this earlier base rose the Chapel in the
middle of the 13th century. The first alteration
made in it was doubtless by Chichele, when the
building of his Water Tower required him to
close up the five lancet windows, which, as in the
east end, adorned the western gable. In doing
so he evidently left in the centre light, a *hagio-*

scope, opening for the use of the occupants of the Tower rooms. For this was substituted by Juxon in 1662 a small bay window, as an ornament, the angel supporting it bearing a shield on which are the arms of that Archbishop.

In Cardinal Morton the Chapel had its chief and most gorgeous beautifier. He filled the windows with stained glass, probably some of the richest which the latter years of the 15th century, so rich in that art, could produce. At every junction of the cross-ribs of the panelled roof were painted in bright colours his monogram or the initial ⅏. And so the Chapel remained until time and neglect had reduced its beautiful windows to the state described by Laud, as being "shameful to look upon, all diversely patched like a beggar's coat." But during that interval an event occurred in connection with this Chapel of historic importance. Archbishop Parker's consecration. Long refuted and exploded though that silly fable concocted by Romanists, known as the "Nag's Head Conspiracy," has been, still an account of this Chapel would incomplete without some reference to it. The story was briefly this: that Archbishop Parker went through a form of consecration at a tavern in Cheapside, bearing that name. This malicious falsehood first saw the light in the pages of a Jesuit named Fitz-Herbert, in the year 1614, about half a century after the event, whereas there were in Lambeth Palace itself, and also in the library of Corpus Christi College, Cambridge, authentic contemporary accounts of the whole scene, describing every detail of place, and persons, and costume, as unanswerable evidence of its truth.

In this Chapel, on the 17th December 1559, was Parker consecrated by four still remaining Bishops, Barlow of Bath, Scory of Hereford, Hodgkins of Bedford, and Miles Coverdale of Exeter. The very locality is described, by the Archbishop himself, "in the Chapel of my Manor of Lambeth," and he goes on to say that after the close of the sermon he " passed through the door on the north side into the vestry," to be robed by his Chaplains. That door is there, and that room still remains, and is to this day used as a vestry.

Another connecting link with the life of Archbishop Parker is to be found in this Chapel. It had been his daily habit to kneel in private prayer on the south side of the Communion

Table, and his desire was often expressed that his bones should find a resting-place there ; for which purpose he had his tomb erected during his life-time.   In that tomb his corpse was duly laid, and there it rested until the days of the Common-wealth, when the Chapel, falling into the hands of Matthew Hardy, was desecrated by feasting and even dancing.   The presence of that tomb, and the consciousness of the corpse within, seemed revolting even to the callous minds of the soldiers, so they broke it open and rifled it, and cast the bones upon a dunghill.

On the Restoration, Archbishop Juxon tried in vain to trace them out, and it was not until Sancroft came to Lambeth that they were recovered.   He once more placed them in the Chapel, in the centre of the floor, with this brief but touching epitaph :—

"CORPUS MATTHEI | ARCHIEPISCOPI | TANDEM HIC QUIESCIT."

Allusion has been made to the state in which Archbishop Laud found the Chapel.   He thus describes it :—" At his coming to Lambeth it lay so nastily, and the windowes were so peeced and quite out of order and reparation, that it grieved his very heart to see it in such a condition."   To repair it was to him a labour of love ; though he

little foresaw that that very act would be
charged against him, and help to bring about his
downfall. The endeavour to restore as far as
he could from the pictures of a " Biblia
Pauperum " the designs which Cardinal Morton
had introduced, aroused the fanaticism of the then
dominant Puritan ; to revive the spirit of devotion
by means of illustrations of Scriptural subjects was
deemed superstition, and denounced as rank
Popery. So not content with destroying
Archbishop Parker's tomb, every window was
demolished and every ornament destroyed.
Juxon, in his almost filial affection for Laud, set
himself to reduce, so far as his short tenure of the
Primacy admitted, the sadly disordered and
dishonoured condition of the Chapel, as he did
also of the Great Hall, and restore it to something of its former beauty ; he filled in the
windows with glass, though not so rich and costly
as that which had been destroyed ; he introduced
oak stalls, with richly carved poppy-heads ; and
everywhere, on the beams of the roof, on the
stalls, on the screen, and over the door, he placed
shields, bearing the arms of his beloved pre-
decessor either alone or impaling those of the See.

In such a state the Chapel had remained, with

only slight alterations and adornment, until
Archbishop Howley succeeded to the Primacy in
1828. His refined classical mind and open-handed
liberality had found in the Palace generally a grand
field for their exercise ; with Mr. Blore, the then
most highly esteemed architect, he set to work to
adapt this noble building to modern requirements,
while jealously retaining all that was historical.
Clearing away two inharmonious and most incon-
venient ranges of private apartments which
successive Archbishops had added on (one after
another), he planned a residence which in its
public and private rooms has few equals. Two
rooms only, Cardinal Pole's Gallery, which faced
the garden, and the quadrangular Library, which
lay by the Guard Room, may possibly raise a
regretful thought ; but even they, only from
historic association, being without a single feature
of architectural beauty worth preserving.

Nor did his Primacy close without the Chapel
experiencing the benefit of his presence. Re-
moving the original flat ceiling, he introduced a
groined arched roof, cleared away the high
panelling on the side walls, which probably
Archbishop Secker had introduced, and thus
brought to light the lower portions of the

windows which had been blocked up, and so gave an air of lightness to the whole building. But it was left to the Primacy of Archbishop Tate to carry still further the work of improvement begun by Archbishop Howley. The plain glass in the windows now gave place to a series of Scriptural subjects in rich stained glass, from the hands of Messrs. Clayton and Bell, according, as far as possible, with those designed by Cardinal Morton; these were contributed by members of the Archbishop's family, and liberal friends. One of them demands special notice. It was dedicated to the memory of Crauford Tate, the Archbishop's son, and was an offering from the American Bishops assembled at the Second Pan-Anglican Synod, in touching remembrance of the visit lately paid by him to the Western branch of the Anglican Church. The Chapel has received further embellishment from the present Archbishop, who has completed the work of wall decoration, and placed on the west wall of the Ante-Chapel the armorial bearings of those of his predecessors whose names were most conspicuous in the annals of the country.

While the eyes of all members of the English Church turn with loving reverence to the old

Palace, in which their Primates have dwelt for some eight centuries, it is to this Chapel especially they look with veneration. Here, for above four centuries, nearly all consecrations of Bishops of the Southern Province were held. Here, too, all the earlier Bishops of the Colonial Church, of India, Canada, the United States, West Indies, Australia, New Zealand, and Africa, received their commission to go forth as " Bishops of the Church of Christ." And their successors are now representing the Apostolic Order and Evangelic Doctrine of their dear Old Mother Church in the remotest regions of the world.

The Dialect of Surrey.

By Granville Leveson Gower, f.s.a.

FEW subjects are more interesting than that of local dialect. It may chance that, as in Yorkshire and in parts of the North of England, it may form a distinct language, unintelligible to any but a native, or it may be as in the South of England that the speech of the common folk, while readily intelligible, is seasoned with a number of dialectal words, some classical, some which were current a century or more ago ; all expressive and all worth treasuring up. It can hardly be said of Surrey that it has any dialect peculiarly its own. It is probable that there is no word in use in the county which is not current in Kent and Sussex, while on the other hand, words are in use in those counties which are not current in Surrey, and a careful perusal of the admirable glossaries of the Rev. W. D. Parish, and of Dr. Pegge, will establish this fact.

When writing, nearly twenty years ago, a paper

on *Surrey Provincialisms* for the English Dialect
Society, I expressed a fear that, in consequence of
increased facilities of travel, and of the spread of
education, these dialect words would disappear
and be forgotten. Old customs, old beliefs, old
prejudices die hard in the soil of England, and I
cannot say that in the rural districts I notice
much difference in the language ; and fresh
provincialisms crop up from time to time. I have
ever noticed that one of the most prolific sources
of supply is to be found in the evidence given by
witnesses before a bench of magistrates. We
have seen before now a judge puzzled by some
local phrase made use of in evidence. And not
so long ago, in the House of Commons, an
ignorant display of irritation was shewn, owing to
a member having employed the word " hind " to
designate an agricultural labourer ; it was supposed
that some stigma attached to this honourable
appellation.

In a paper of this kind it is impossible to do
more than give instances culled from different
sources to illustrate the local phraseology. It is
unfortunate that many books, which purport to
deal with local dialect, mix up the language of
different counties in hopeless confusion ; the

works of George Eliot, *Field Paths and Green Lanes*, by the late L. Jennings, and that incomparable little work, by the late Rev. J. Coker Egerton, *Sussex Folk and Sussex Ways*, of which a reprint has happily recently been issued, and *Chronicles of a Clay Farm*, by Chandos Wren Hoskyns, these may be relied upon as absolutely trustworthy.

There are not many proverbs specially belonging to Surrey. "A bright Candlemas Day" is taken to denote a probable renewal of winter, this was the account given to me by an old man :— "The old folks used to say that so far as the sun shone [the 'o' in the word pronounced long] into the house on Candlemas Day, so far would the snow drive in before the winter was out." A fine Easter Day is supposed to be followed by "plenty of grass, but little good hay ;" meaning that the summer will be wet. A fine bark-harvest, *i.e.*, fine weather for getting in the bark after the oak "flawing" is done, indicates fine weather for gathering in the harvest. "I expect," said a farmer, "we shall have a shuckish time at harvest, we had it so at bark-harvest, and they generally follow one another."

There is a prejudice against thunder early in

the year, hence the saying " Early thunder, late hunger." The black-thorn winter or black-thorn "hatch" as it is sometimes called, is always spoken of to denote the cold weather which generally prevails about the time that the black-thorn is in bloom. A backward spring is thought to indicate a fruitful season ; the common people have this proverb :—

> " When the cuckoo comes to a bare thorn,
>   Then there's like to be plenty of corn."

The point from which the wind blows at any quarter day, is supposed to denote that it will remain more or less in the same quarter for the ensuing three months, and the same is said with regard to Kingston Fair Day, which occurs on 13th November. A writer in *Notes and Queries* (vi. s., ii., 406) gives a remark made to him, " The wind's a-blowing hard from the south-west, and wherever she is this day, she'll stick to all the winter." The moon is supposed to govern the weather absolutely, the time of day at which it changes is all-important, the nearer midnight the better, the nearer mid-day the worse. The prejudice against a new moon on a Saturday is universal, and finds expression in the following doggrel :—

"Saturday new and Sunday full,
  Ne'er brought good and never shall." (pronounced "shull.")

Another weather proverb is, "So many fogs in March, so many frostĕs in May."

The "pig in the poke" is the proverb for an untried bargain, in Surrey as elsewhere; to "talk his dog's hind leg off" is to be an incessant talker, this proverb exists elsewhere as "to talk a horse's leg off." Returning from Croydon one winter night, a remark was made as to the excessive darkness, when the driver replied, "Aye, so it is, dark as Newgate Knocker."

"A dark Christmas makes a heavy wheat-sheaf," *i.e.*, when there is no moonlight at Christmas, it betokens a good harvest. A green Christmas, *i.e.*, one without frost or snow, is said to be followed by a full churchyard, being regarded as unhealthy.

"Deaf as a beetle" does not refer, as might be supposed, to the insect of that name, but is equivalent to "deaf as a post," "beetle" or "biddle" being used in Surrey for a mallet.

"Christen your own child first" was the somewhat forcible way, in which a local Poor Law guardian expressed the sentiment that charity begins at home.

"Too big for my fireplace," is equivalent to "beyond my means." It was used to me thus, " Thank you for letting me look at the farm, but I think it is too big for my fireplace."

An old man who had been neglected by a worthless son, remarked to me plaintively, "It ain't often that the young birds feed the old."

Where we should say of an over-busy man that he had "too many irons in the fire," a Surrey man would say that he had too many "heats" in the fire. As "heats" is used here as a substantive, so they use "hot" as a verb; they say of a thing that they will "hot" it over the fire.

Surrey is not especially rich in folk-lore, but a certain number of superstitions linger here as elsewhere. A death in the family is duly announced to the bees; it is supposed that rain is wanted on St. Swithun's Day to "christen the apples," otherwise there will be no fruit.*

Not so many years ago I knew an instance of an infant, who was badly ruptured, being passed through a holly tree as a charm. The process was the following, a slit was made in the tree, the parts of which were held asunder by two persons, while two women, one holding the child's head,

---

* See *Notes and Queries,* 6. S. iv., 67.

and the other his feet, passed him stark naked several times backwards and forwards through the opening, and my informant added that the mark could be seen in the bark of the tree, and remarked "I don't know that it was any good, but the old women at that time used to hold with it." It is believed that a cake baked on Good Friday will keep any length of time, and not become mouldy, or "mothery" as they express it. An old man told me that thirty years or more ago his wife had baked a cake on Good Friday, and hung it up by a string, that ten or twelve years afterwards it was quite good, and that he had eaten it in sop; he said further "if you grate it and put it in gruel, it is a fine thing for the inside," meaning as a remedy for diarrhœa. This superstition is mentioned by Brand in his *Popular Antiquities* (Hazlitt's Edition, vol. i., p. 88).

The like tradition as to its power to keep fresh, attaches to water caught on Ascension Day. The same man told me that "if you ketch'd the rain water as it fell on Holy Thursday, and put it in a bottle and corked it, you might keep it as long as you would, and it would never go bad."

I knew a case lately where, as a cure for

4

whooping cough, a woman hollowed out a nut and put a spider in it, and hung it by a string round her child's neck, the idea being that when the spider dies the whooping cough disappears with it. The Rev. W. D. Parish mentions this as a cure for ague (*Sussex Dialect,* p. 64).

It is believed that the moss, or "comb" (pronounced "coom"), which collects on church bells is a cure for the shingles. I enquired one day the reason of my carter boy's absence, and the farm-man replied, "He has got the shingles, and I have told his father to get the 'comb' of the church bells and rub it into him; they say it's the best thing for it."

To pass now to the dialect itself.

"A" is used generally before substantives, adjectives, and participles, *e.g.,* a-plenty, a-many, a-coming, a-going. We retain it still in the phrase "going a-begging." "I see you 'a' listening to the nightingale," said the hedge-cutter, "there be 'a' plenty of 'em," are phrases which occur in Jenning's *Field Paths;* speaking also of the healthiness of the Surrey hills, it is not uncommon to hear "people live here as long as they've 'a' mind to."

Double negatives in a sentence, or for the

matter of that as many as can be crammed in, are universal. " You don't know nothing of my dooties noways," was a remark made in my hearing; " You don't gather up no stoans with this ;" and "The gent ain't going to give us nothing," are illustrations from *Field Paths.* The definition of a hypocrite in *Sussex Folks* (p. 13), besides its appropriateness, is an illustration in point, " When a man walks lame as hasn't got nothin' the matter wi' him !" " Blesh ye, them Romans and Antidaluvians don't know no more about farming than a lot o' cockney tailors " (*Chronicles of a Clay Farm*, p. 178). Instances might be adduced also from Chaucer and Shakespeare.

" Be " is general for " are." " How 'be' you ?" is the morning's greeting, to which " I 'be' pretty middlin', thank ye," is the usual answer. The A.V. in St. John, viii. 33, has, " We 'be' Abraham's seed ;" " They beënt practical farmers as writes that stuff," is from *Chronicles of a Clay Farm*, p. 91. "You've no ought" is equivalent to, " You ought not to." Comparatives are formed by adding " er" to the positive, and " est " to the superlative, where, in ordinary speech, we should use " more " and " most," *e.g.*, " a 'picksomer' child (*i.e.*, daintier) there can't be," "He's the 'impudentest chap I ever see;" "She'll get busier and 'mischievouser' every day." (*Silas Marner*, ch. xiv. 108). Double comparatives are very common; of some new cows which I had bought, the cowman said, "They are higher, more upstandinger than ou'rn." Similarly with superlatives. A man will say, "This is the most 'terrifyest' job I ever had." "More happier" and "most boldest" are used by Shakespeare, and the A.V. has "the most 'straightest' sect" (Acts, xxvi. 5). "The minister of the Gospel may be more learneder" (Hooke's *Eccl. Pol.:* Bk. vii., ch. iii. 1, p. 1197).

"Grow'd," "know'd," "see'd," "throw'd," and such like forms are used both for the perfect and participle passive of the verbs. "How the swedes have grow'd to be sure on that piece as we drained last year" (*Chronicles of a Clay Farm*, p. 90). "I've 'know'd' a litter of seven whelps reared in that hole" (*Id.*, p. 44). "They throw a word to you when they do speak, as if they 'throw'd' a bone to a dog" (*Field Paths*, 169). The word "throw" is also used in a peculiar sense of being sold or disappointed in a bargain. "I got 'throwed' over that job."

"See" is used also as the preterite for "saw,"

so in *Pickwick*, "I 'see' her a kissin' of him agin."

"Rose," "took," and "wrote" are participles passive for "risen," "taken," and "written." "We shall get rain, I doubt, for after the sun had 'rose' he went to bed again." "Took wus" is invariable for "taken ill." "Don't mind her, sir, said he, she was 'took' so at two years old" (*Field Paths*, p. 10). "He hasn't 'wrote' never since he left home."

Past participles are formed in "ded," "ted," *e.g.* attackted, drownded, which latter has the classical authority of Dickens. "To the wery top, sir?" inquired the waiter. "Why the milk will be drownded." "Never you mind that," replied Mr. Squeers, "serve it right for being so dear" (*Nicholas Nickleby*, c. v., p. 35.)

"Such a country as this, where everything is either scorched up with the sun or 'drownded' with the rain." (Man near Dorking, *Field Paths*, *etc.*, p. 141.)

"The mare 'foalded' last night."

"The old pond bay is terrible out o' Kelter, it's got reg'lar 'underminded' by the water." "The plaäce is 'underminded' by rats."

Certain words are invariably mispronounced.

It may be well to give a list of some of them :—

Acrost for across; agoo for ago; batcheldor for bachelor; brownchitis (or sometime brown titus) for bronchitis; chimley or chimbley for chimney; crowner for coroner; crowner's quest for coroner's inquest; curosity and curous for curiosity and curious; death for deaf; disgest for digest, and indisgestion for indigestion; gownd for gown; scholard for scholar; nevvy for nephew; non-plush'd for non-plussed; refuge for refuse; quid for cud, "chewing the quid;" sarment for sermon; varmint for vermin; sloop for slope; spartacles for spectacles; spavin for spasms. I knew an old woman who was constantly suffering from "the windy spavin;" taters for potatoes; wunst for once; wuts for oats, etc., etc.

The pleonastic use of like, in such phrases as comfortable-'like,' timid-'like,' dazed-'like,' deserves notice. "I have felt lonesome-'like' ever since." (*Field Paths, etc.,* p. 23.) "The farmer's work was over-'like." (*Chronicles of a Clay Farm,* p. 90.)

The use of "of," after the verb is peculiar. They will say I found "of" him, I missed "of" it, etc., so "tell of" "they was 'telling of' it the other night at Bogmoor" (*Chronicles of a Clay Farm*, p. 135.)*

The vagaries of the verb " to be " are manifold. We "am," they "am," we "was," they "was," are constantly heard, and similarly, I "are," I "were," we " is," etc. One day in covert shooting, we challenged the beater on the left, "Where are you George !" The answer came back, " Here I 'are,' all on the standstill." The reply to a question put to a witness at the Bench, " You are a labourer I believe," was, " Yes sir, I 'are.'" " You know we 'is,'" was another answer noted at the same place. These peculiarities are well illustrated in the following, from *Field Paths, etc.* (p. 28, 169, 211) :—" Bricks 'is ' scarce." " They 'has' to be idle." "We 'has' artists down here." "I 'has' enough to do." These last instances show a similar disregard to singulars and plurals in respect of other verbs. The possessive pronouns are invariably "hern," "hisn," "ourn," and "yourn;" " his-self " and " theirselves " do duty for himself and themselves, rightly as nominatives, but also as accusatives, *e.g.*, " he hurt 'hisself,'" " the

* This use of " of " occurs in Dr. South's *Sermons* (Sermon iv., 431) "which none ever missed ' of ' who came up to the conditions of it."

horse stabbed 'hisself' somehow." There is a peculiar use of "me," which still survives in ordinary language in "methinks," in the word "mesure," for I am sure. "I don't know 'mesure.'"

We now give examples of some dialectal words, and perhaps it will be best to place them in alphabetical order. I give merely a selection of the most noticeable examples out of a great many.

"Along of," "all along of." In consequence of. "How did sin come into the world?" was the question put to a Sunday school boy. "'All along of' Eve eating that there apple," was the prompt reply. Foster uses it in his *Life of Dickens* (vol. iii., 79). " And to be in difficulties 'all along of' this place which he has planted with his own hands."

"Agate," going on in making. " I worked on the railway when the new line was 'agate.'"

"Anyways," in anyway. "For if the child ever went 'anyway's' wrong." *(Silas Marner,* c. xiv., p. 108.)

"Appeal to," approve of. I asked a man how he found his whisky suit him, and he answered, " I 'appeal to' it very much."

"Argify," *i.e.*, signify, or matter. "It don't 'argify' much which way you does it."

"Bait." The afternoon or four o'clock meal in hay and harvest time. A Surrey labourer's meals are his breakfast, his bever or eleven o'clock meal, his lunch the mid-day meal, his bait, and his supper.

"Bannick," to beat or thrash. I heard one boy say to another during a storm, "If you go and get wet, you'll get a 'bannicking' when you go home." There are numberless other words to express the same thing, *e.g.*, "hide," "fight," "jacket," "leather."

"Baulky" is said of a person who avoids you, keeps out of your way. "I saw the prisoner look rather 'baulky,'" said a police-constable in evidence.

"Beazled," tired out. "That young 'meer' (mare) was properly 'beazled' after they journeys in the coal team." "Jowled out" is used in the same sense.

"Befront" is in front of. "He was walking about ten yards 'befront.'" "We keep driving of it all 'befront' of us," said a quarryman.

"Beleft" is the participle of believe. "I never could have 'beleft' that he would have bested us so."

"Bettermost," pronounced "bettamy." People of the upper classes are described as "'bettamy' kind of folks." Another expression of the same kind is "carriage folks;" "A pedestrian's luncheon not fit for what the people call 'carriage folks,'" "Just below the church are some old cottages, and some 'carriage folks'' houses are in or near the village" *(Field Paths,* pages 139, 173).

"Bitten," used adjectively. A dog is said to be "bitten" when he is given to bite.

"Bly," a likeness. "He has a 'bly' of his father" means that he is rather like him. The more usual expression is to "favour," which implies a strong resemblance. This is not strictly a local word, and occurs in Shakespeare, *The Spectator,* etc. "St. Louis is a very blood-like colt 'favouring' another son of Hermit, Peter," is an extract from the sporting intelligence of the *Times.*

"Brave" is a constant epithet of things large or fine, whether animate or inanimate ; a "brave" beast, a "brave" oak, etc. "I went to see my grandsons, and carried them a 'brave' basket of nectarines," occurs in one of the Hon. Mrs. Boscawen's letters ; and Dickens, in one of his letters, speaks of some " brave " old churches on the Rhine.

" Burden," quantity. " There aint a great ' burden ' of grass this year."

" Call," occasion, need. " Especially as you've no ' call ' to be told how to value yourself, my dear," says Mr. Boffin in Dickens' *Mutual Friend;* " You've no ' call ' to catch cold " *(Silas Marner*, ch. xiii., 102) ; " And here there is no ' call ' even to regret how great an actor was in Dickens lost " *(Life of Dickens*, vol. ii., 181).

" Cant over," to upset, *e.g.*, " The wagon ' canted over.' "

" Caterways," " catering," and the verb to " cater," signify to cross diagonally. One is often directed to cross a field " caterways ;" a drain which crosses a hill diagonally instead of going straight down it is said to " cater " the hill.

" Christian," human being. " I never see sich a dog, he's as sensible as any ' Christian.' "

" Clung," moist, damp. Grass which has been exposed to wet is said to handle so " clung."

" Denial," drawback. Mr. Parish quotes " his deathness is a great ' denial ' to him." The same idea is expressed by the word " hurt."

" Dignify," identify. In a larceny case the

witness said : " Amongst the three I ' dignified ' this man."

" Dishabill." This word must have come down as a legacy, I think, from the Norman-French waiting-maids. The inmate of a cottage will tell you " We're all in ' dishbill' this morning," if she has not had time to clean the house ; " Our churchyard aint 'tended to as it were in Muster Bigg's time, it's all in ' dishbill' now," said a sexton who was showing me over a church. Other French words have, we know, been retained : the countryman calls the fox Reynolds, from the French renard; and when the butcher talks of the " costes " of a sheep or bullock, it is the French *côte a side*; while obedience for a bow or curtsey is, of course, from *obeisance.* It was re-freshing the other day to hear from an old man who complained of being blind, " It hurts me so that I can't see your carriage when it passes to make my ' obedience.' "

" Dout " is to do out, put out. " As soon as I see it was a fire I done my best to ' dout' it ;" " I'll be sure and ' dout' it afore I goo."

" Druv," driven. " I won't be ' druv' " is a favourite expression in Surrey. The crest attributed to Sussex is a hog, and the motto,

"We wun't be 'druv'" (Egerton, *Sussex Folks and Sussex Ways*, page 7).

"Dryth," drought. During the present season we have heard often enough of the "dryth." Of trees planted in a loose soil, it is said they must be trod up or the "dryth" will get into them.

"Ellow." If a plum pudding, or what they call a "pond-butter pudding," is very short of currants, or has but few plums in it, they say it is "terrible 'ellow.'" The word is possibly connected with "ellinge," lonely. "It's a nice pleasant place in summer, but in winter it's unaccountable cold and 'ellinge,'" said a woman who lived on the hill.

"To fail" is to fall ill, generally of some infectious illness, *e.g.*, "to fail" with the measles, or the "glass-pock," which is the name given to chicken-pox.

"Fitty" is subject to fits.

"Fight" is used in the sense of to beat.

"To flaw," literally "to flay," is to take the bark off; the "flawing time" is the oak-barking season. "I've got a very bad cold, almost as if I was 'flawed,' so sore inside;" "All that the shepherd said when they told him some more of the lambs were dead was, 'Then there'll be a lot more for me to "flaw," I reckon.'" Dickens writes: "Till I have been 'flayed' with the cold."

A "flittermouse" is a bat.

A "fly-golding" a lady-bird, or "lady-bug," as it is called.

"Foundrous," bottomless, boggy. "The road over the common is too 'foundrous' in this wet weather."

"Fruz" is the past participle of freeze. "I got regular 'fruz' from the cold."

"Going home," figuratively said of a tree when it is decaying. "That old tree's 'gwain home' very fast. A writer in *Notes and Queries* (5 f., vi., 126) says that his gardener, speaking of some plants which showed little signs of life, said, "I was afraid they were 'gone home.'"

The church bell "goes out" when it tolls. "I heer'd the church bell 'go out' for someone to-day."

The principal house in a place, although it may not be very large, is always called the "great-house." "We be a-goin' to kill him after dinner for the 'great-house'" (*Field Paths*, p. 148).

A "gratten" is a stubble, whether of corn, peas, or beans; the clover-leys also are called the "sheep-grattens." Partridges feeding on the stubbles, or pigs turned out there, are said to be " grattening."

" Hand " is a trouble or handful. " It's a very great ' hand ' to have sich a long family." " First hands " is at first starting.

To " hele," or " hele in " a building, is to cover it with straw or tiles ; mangold or potatos are " heled " up when they are covered with earth. In Wiclif's translation of the Bible (1 Cor., xi.) the word " helid " occurs throughout where the A.V. has " covered," *e.g.,* " Bisemeth it a woman ' helid ' on the head to praise God " (v. 13).

A " hem " is used expletively for a quantity. " I see a ' hem ' of a lot of sand mucked out there sureligh." No more amusing instance is given of the use of the word than that in *Sussex Folks and Sussex Ways,* p. 3 :—" Politics are about like this," said a Sussex man, " I've got a sow in my yard with twelve little uns, and they little uns can't all feed at once, so I shut six on 'em out of the yard while t'other six be sucking, and the six as be shut out they just do make a ' hem ' of a noise till they be let in, and then they be just as quiet as the rest."

" Innardly." Of a person who mumbles, it is said " he talks so ' innardly.' "

"Interrupt." This word is used not only of interfering with or attacking, but also in the sense of causing discomfort, disagreeing with. "If I eats any heavy food it 'interrupts' me so."

"Jacket." A workman always calls his coat a jacket.

"Jack up." A very common word in the sense of stopping, refusing to work any more. "That spring 'most always 'jacks up' in autumn time."

"Jiniver" is the pronunciation of January, and seems to come very near the French. There is a prejudice against hatching chickens in January. "'Jiniver' poults never come to no good," said the old poultry woman.

"Joy" is the pronunciation of the bird known as the jay.

"Kings' evil." The scrofula is still known by this name.

"Leastways" is a word perpetually in use. "Everybody's rich over there, or, 'leastways,' its their own fault if they aint" (*Field Paths*, p. 170).

In the "lew," pronounced loo, is in the shelter, or in the leuth as a substantive, the verb to lew is to shelter or protect from the rain.

"Lief," "Liever." "I'd as lief not," I would rather not. "I had as 'lief' my tailor should sew

gingerbread nuts on my coat instead of buttons."
(Cowper's *Letters*, No. 55).

Gower's noble sentiment must be quoted (Conf.
Amant. Lib., 1.)—

> " The knight had 'lever' for to die
> Than breke his trouth."

" Lippy," insolent. " A very 'lippy' man " is
a man who insults you.

" Looses " are the deep ruts in a cartway.

" Market fresh," one of the many euphemisms for
drunk. Rev. W. Parish, *Sussex Dialect*, p. 30,
gives a curious Sussex expression, " concerned in
drink." It is impossible ever to get an admission
of drunkenness,—" he'd had a drop of beer" is
about as far as one can get.

" Messengers " are the flying clouds which
detach themselves from the rest, and float across
the sky. They are called also water dogs, and are
sure indications of wet weather.

" Middling " is a word which does duty in
various senses. If you enquire of a countryman
how he does, or of a farmer how his crops are
looking, you never get beyond " middling " in
reply. " He's given to chuck people out
'middling' sudden," said a witness speaking of a
publican.

"Mixen" is a heap of dung and soil, or other compost. The story of "Master Wimber," told in *Sussex Folks*, p. 15, and how he should spend his holiday after twenty years' hard work, affords a charming picture of rustic contentment. "He would buy four ounces of baccer, and sit on the 'mixen,' and smoke it out."

"Native," birthplace or native place used as a substantive.

"No out." This is the verdict of the rustic umpire, instead of "not out." A great deal of dialect is to be heard in a cricket tent. "Holt," "Holt," is shouted to an incautious batsman if attempting a short run ; and if an appeal is made for a catch from a ball that touches the ground, a chorus of "Cowden, first bounce out," is in this district shouted out by the spectators. It is clear that in some match in which Cowden, a village in Kent, on the south-east border of Surrey, was engaged, the umpire had given a man out first "bounce," and the tradition lingers still. The remark is always received with much merriment

"Noration" or "oration," an unnecessary fuss or to-do about anything. "He made quite a 'noration' down the valley from public-house to public-house," said a police constable in a case of drunkenness.

"Nurt." To entice, to lead astray, also nourish. "The cat got up in the tree, and we did all we could to 'nurt' her down." In a dog-stealing case, the witness being asked whether the defendants were discouraging the dog from following, answered :—"They was 'nurting' of it all they could." Speaking of young cattle, the farm man said, "We must 'nurt' 'em along a little bit."

"Order." To be in a tidy order about anything is to be very much put out.

"Ordinary," pronounced "ornary," said of persons who are unwell, and of crops which are scanty. "I feel plaguy 'ornary,' I can tell 'ee."

"Otherwhile." Every now and then, occasionally. "I takes a glass of beer 'otherwhile.'"

"Outasked" is to have had the banns of marriage published three times. "I agreed to marry them on the Monday morning after they were 'outasked'" (*Sussex Folk*, p. 96).

"Out and out" is a favourite expression for first-rate. "They tell me that the last turkey I sent in was an 'out and out' 'un."

"Out o' doors." This is used in various ways; "Farming is gone 'out o' doors,'" *i.e.*, has gone to the bad; "I don't know many of these plants about, they be 'out o' doors' now," *i.e.*, have gone out of fashion; "There's not a better field lies 'out' o' doors,'" said the woodman, and with this compare, "There'll never be standing still for winter work on this here farm, as long as ever it lies 'out o' doors,' let who will farm it!" (*Chronicles of a Clay Farm*, p. 90.)

"Peart," pronounced as a dissyllable, brisk, lively. "I'm 'pert' and willing to listen to his proposal of a journey." (Letter of Hon. Mrs. Boscawen, March 11th, 1794). "I preached for him three times, and one of his parishioners was kind enough to say, 'Your father, sir, is the "peartest" old gentleman I ever seed.'" (*Life of Dean Hook*, ii., p. 492.)

"Picksome," dainty, of a delicate appetite.

"Pick upon," to interefere with or annoy. "I think it very hard for me to be 'picked upon' always."

"Plaguey," an expletive. "I feel 'plaguey' queer," or "'plaguey' ornary," *i.e.*, "I am very unwell."

> "And yet methinks to tell you true
>   You sell it 'plaguey' dear."
>
> (Cowper.   *Yearly distress in Tithing Time at Stock, Essex*).

"Play upon," always of pain. "The toothache 'played upon' me so, that I was nearly drove distracted."

"Platty," uneven. "The hops is wonderful 'platty' this year."

"Pretty," used adverbially, "nicely." They will say to a child, "Speak 'pretty' to the gentleman." "The boy sings 'pretty,' don't he, Master Marner?" "Yes," said Silas, absently, "very 'pretty.'" (*Silas Marner*, x., 74.)

"Puddle about," to walk about slowly as an old man, or as one recovering from an illness. "He jist 'puddles about' in the garden when 'tis fine."

"Pull," to summons before the Bench. "He's bin that disagree'ble ever sin I 'pulled' him that time."

"Put upon," to impose upon. "I'll not be 'put upon' by no man." (*Silas Marner*, ch. xi., p. 40).

"Quirk," to make a faint noise indicative of fear. Of a rabbit in a hole when worried by a ferret, and preparing to bolt, the man said, "I hear 'un rumble, aint he jist a 'quirking.'"

"Round-Frock," a smock-frock, otherwise a "slop." There are still two men in my own parish (Titsey) who wear them, but in another generation they will have become things of the past.

"Rowen," the grass after mowing, or the second crop. "He said he wouldn't be in a hurry as he'd had two 'rowen' stacks fired in his time."

> "The other forbeare
> For 'rowen' to spare."
>   —(Tusser's *Husbandry*, 56, 25.)

"Runagate," a good-for-nothing fellow. "One of they 'runagate' chaps." "Ay, they be 'runagates,'" *i.e.*, "ne'er-do-wells" (*Field Paths*, p. 38).

"Runt," locally a Welsh bullock. "Heriot unus boviculus Anglicè a 'runt'" (*Court Roll, Titsey Manor*, 23 May, 1715).

"Saturday night," weekly pay. "He's troubled to find work for his men this snowy weather, and they all expect their 'Saturday night' jist the same."

"Sauce," pronounced "soss," vegetables; called also "green soss."

"Scrow," sulky, scowling. "He looked very 'scrow' at me."

"Set," settle. "I had no food all day, and took some cider, and a little whisky on the top of it, and it didn't set well." [Defendant's answer to a charge of drunkenness].

"Shatter," a sprinkling, or fair crop. "There be a middlin' 'shatter' o' hops this year, I reckon."

"Sheers," the shires so pronounced. Any one not living in Kent, Surrey, or Sussex is described as "coming from the sheers." "This word," says Rev. J. C. Egerton (*Sussex Folks*, p. 19), "a non-Sussex reader may interpret to mean any part of England generally outside of Sussex, Surrey, or Kent." The pronunciation is illustrated by the following epitaph in Deddington Church, Oxon., on Thomas Greenhill, died 1634 :—

> "Under thy feete interr'd is here,
> A Native borne in Oxford-shere."

"Shifty," untidy, helpless. "She was a wonderful 'shifty' woman," was the description of a farmer's untidy wife.

"Shuckish," showery, unsettled ; of weather.

"Shut of." To get rid of. An old gardener was complaining of the young ladies of a family who were very numerous, for making constant raids upon his fruit. One of them said to him, "Why ! Masters, how thankful you ought to be that we are not all boys." "Ne'er a bit, miss," he answered, "for if ye were boys ye'd but be at home for the holidays, and then I should get 'shut' o' ye."

"Sight," a great quantity, a great deal. "There's a wonderful 'sight' o' apples this year." "It costës a 'sight' o' money." "We catch a 'sight' of fish" (*Field Paths*, iii., 11). "It did her a 'sight' o' good" (*Chronicles of a Clay Farm*, p. 92).

"Smoke, up in the," *i.e.*, in London. To prisoner, "Where have you been since December last?" "I've been up in the smoke."

"Snob." A cobbler, travelling shoemaker.

"Spilt." Spoiled. "If you've got anything as can be 'spilt' or broke" (*Silas Marner*, ch. xiv., 108).

> "Who-so will it knowe
> Who-so spareth the spyrnge
> 'Spilleth' his children."
>
> —*Piers Plowman.*

"Spoon-meat." Broth or slops. "He's not taken nothin' but 'spoon-meat' for ever so long."

"Statesman." A landowner. "It's all very well for you 'statesmen' to keep oak trees for the pleasure of looking at 'em."

"Stood." Stuck fast. "The wagon got stood there."

"Stud." A state of meditation, a brown study. "I met Mr. Jones, but he seemed all in a 'stud,' and not to take no notice o' what I said."

"Swimy," giddy, light-headed, pronounced with 'i' long. " What can be more picturesque," asks a Sussex correspondent, " than our bailiff's account of his attack of influenza." " Well, sir, I felt that 'swimy I seem'd most ready to pitch otherwhile."

"Team," not restricted to horses, *e.g.*, " a 'team' of cows."

"Terrify," pronounced "tarrify," to tease or annoy. A child who asks for a thing over and over again is said "to keep all on 'terrifying.'" A cough is "terrifying." A batsman who hits hard is said to "terrify" the bowler.

"Tidy," in sense of good, well. "He's getting along pretty 'tidy.'" "Our paärson is a very 'tidy' preacher," said a clerk who was shewing me over a church; the same man remarked, "that's our warming 'apparition'" (*i.e.*, "apparatus.")

"Timmersome," timid.

"Tissick," a tickling cough.

"Trapes about." To go about in a shipshod, untidy manner.

"Travish," rubbish, refuse.

"Unaccountable." No word is more frequently on the lips of the labourer. "Work is 'unaccountable' slack just now."

"Up," to get up hurriedly, or lift passionately. "He 'ups' with his fist."

"Up-grown," grown up. "We never get about eight or ten 'up-grown' persons at church in the morning."

"Uppards." He lives "uppards" means in direction of London. The wind is 'uppards,' implies that it is in the North.

"Upset," to find fault with, attack, or knock down. "I didn't like to tackle him because there were two of 'em, and I was afraid he would 'upset' me."

"Venturesome," adventurous.

"Victuals," pronounced also "wittles," food generally. "I'll just get a bit o' 'vittles,' and then I'll be off."

"Warrant," pronounced "warn't." "He'll not be long there, I'll 'warn't' ye."

"Week-a-days," as distinguished from Sunday. "I wears it Sundays and 'week-a-days.'"

"Welt," or "welt-up," scorched. "The grass is reg'lar 'welted' this year."

"Wift," quick and silently. I was walking with a man, and a bicycle passed us without our hearing it, and he said, "They come by so 'wift,' don't they?"

"Wonderful," excessively, of German "wunderbar." "'Wonderful' weak," "'wonderful' hot," etc. "I've seen men as are 'wonderful' handy wi' children" (*Silas Marner*, ch. xiv., 107.) The following recommendation of her future son-in-law was given to me by a cottager, together with the account of his courtship :—"I don't know no harm of the young man, he hung on constant to Hemma for seven year, and walked out with her sister afore that, and he's a 'wonderful' handy chap to carry water."

"Wore out," worn out. "Yes, I'm cripplish 'wore out,' that's all." "Poor thing, she was fairly 'wore out'" (*Field Paths*, p. 69).

"Yaffle," the green woodpecker, so called from its laughing note.

"Year," plural for "years." "That's my own mother, and she be dead sixty 'year.'" "I was a sawyer up in them woods for five and forty 'year'" (*Field Paths*, p. 40, 137).

Such are some of the provincialisms yet to be heard in Surrey ; many of them are peculiar to the South of England, others are current elsewhere. I have given nothing which I have not heard myself from the mouths of the inhabitants, and the illustrations which I have supplied, except where taken from books, are such as have been used in conversation with me. They tell us of the language of our forefathers, and as such are a contribution to " Bygone Surrey."

Ancient Roads and Ways.

By H. F. Napper.

THE WATLING STREET.—In treating of the ancient roads and ways of Bygone Surrey, the old Watling Street claims, of course, the first notice. But the question arises whether in the earliest times that part of Surrey through which this road runs was not a portion of Kent; for the boundary between Surrey and Kent was at one time so uncertain that in the seventeenth century there was a solemn inquiry by the Judges to decide whether Hatcham was part of Surrey or of Kent; and it was decided to be in Surrey.

Ptolemy says distinctly that Londinium belonged to the Cantii. The origin of the Roman name of Londinium would appear to be the British name Llong Dinas, which probably means a place for ships. I have often wondered why the Welshmen always write their name Llan with two l's, when one would be sufficient; but lately I have observed that the oldest writers write the word Lhan, so that I imagine the second l is now

intended to represent h; therefore apparently
Llong Dinas should be Lhong Dinas; but the
Romans dropped the h and g as surplusage, and
made the name Londinium. Well, then, if
Londinium belonged to the Cantii, their
territory must have extended beyond the present
bounds of Kent; and it would follow that
Londinium was located on the south side of the
Thames, in what is now the county of Surrey;
for it is most improbable that the Trinobantes
would allow the Cantii to have a town on their
side of the river; but nevertheless the Trinobantes might have a town, or some settlement of
their own, on their side; and, indeed, this would
appear quite probable, for the remains of pile
dwellings have been found in the peat of
Finsbury, as well as of Southwark; and the part
of Surrey which belonged to Kent would probably be represented by Southwark, Bermondsey,
and perhaps Lambeth, which extends a long way
down towards Kent. The neighbours of the
Cantii were the Rhemi, who inhabited East
Surrey perhaps as far as the river Wey, where
they adjoined the Bibroci. I say, then, that
Londinium of the Cantii was on the south side
of the Thames; but it has been objected that this

was too wet and marshy a place for the British
town. We know, however, that the Britons
relied on their marshes for protection against
invaders (perhaps wolves), and therefore made
their dwellings in marshy and woody places; but
this locality was not all marsh, for we find
Bermonds Eye and Horse Eye included in it,
shewing there were islets of higher ground interspersed between the marshes and creeks, whereon
they could dwell in safety and comfort.

We know, now, that the Watling Street ran
from the coast of Kent to London, and crossed
the Thames there; and we know further that
above 150 years before the time of Ptolemy,
Julius Cæsar made a second raid into Kent; and
Mr. Vine, in his book, "Cæsar in Kent,"
conducts him up the Watling Street as far as
about Dartford, which is no doubt correct; but
from that point he takes him to Holwood Hill,
by what may have been afterwards a road to
Noviomagus; and thence across the heaths and
wilds of Surrey (by unknown tracks) to Coway
Stakes on the Thames, where Camden fancied he
had found the locality of his crossing by the
implication of the "Stakes" which had been
found there, and which he identified with the

stakes said to have been used by the Britons to
fortify the ford to which they retreated, and
where they intended to resist the crossing of
Cæsar and his army.

But it is much more likely that, if the Britons
(with their 4,000 chariots) retreated along the
Watling Street so far as Dartford, they would
continue their retreat along the same road, and
not (with their chariots) across pathless heaths
and wilds of Surrey to Coway Stakes.

We know that the Watling Street crossed the
Thames and ran on to St. Albans (and far
beyond); but the point for consideration is where,
at what spot, was the "ford" which the Britons
had fortified with stakes, and there awaited the
coming of Cæsar? It can scarcely be supposed
to be elsewhere than on or near the line of the
road by which the Britons were retreating; and it
is remarkable that in the very line of their retreat,
where the river is widest, and therefore most
shallow, there is on the Middlesex bank a locality
called "Hungerford," near Charing Cross.

And from the Lambeth side of the river, opposite to Hungerford, may be traced by the names
of the Narrow Wall and Pedlar's Acre (Agger) a
route from this ford to Londinium at Southwark

and Bermondsey. And further, on the Middlesex side, the ancient Saltway to Londinium may be traced from Uxbridge, *via* Acton, Kensington, and Hyde Park,* straight to this ford. And I observe what is very remarkable, that Mr. Vine, in the first map in his book "Cæsar in Kent," actually carries the Watling Street up to the bend in the Thames, opposite Hungerford, and not to Westminster Bridge, where it is usually thought to have crossed. Why was this done? I say, then, very confidently, that *this* was the *ford* where Cæsar dislodged the Britons and crossed the Thames.

I am aware that Dr. Guest says that the crossing was at Halliford, because he thinks that was the lowest ford down the river; but Hungerford is clearly far lower down, and also is on Cæsar's probable line of march on the Watling Street. Yet it is remarkable that although a market was established by its side, the ford became disused in the course of time, and for this reason :—

When the Romans had established themselves in Britain, they soon settled a new colony at Londinium; but this was on the north side of

* Rotton Row, the fashionable ride, seems to be the old Roman road.

6

the river, on the site of the present city of
London, and it was called " Londinium Augusta."
And when this had been done it was apparently
found convenient to divert the Watling Street
from its old course to Hungerford into the new
colony (probably by means of a ferry) at London
Bridge; from this we have the Watling Street of
to-day within the city; and it was carried on to
Hampsted, and into the main line again near
Hendon: and it would appear that they
straightened the course of the main line from
about the Paragon in Kent Road over the river
at Lambeth Ferry, and by the Edgeware Road
to the camp at Brockley Hill (Sulloniacæ); and
these two diversions together rendering the ford
at Hungerford less necessary, and probably less
used, it by degrees became disused and forgotten
altogether.

That the fact was as stated can be readily seen
by the Ravenna list of names, where, coming up
the Watling Street from Durobrivæ (Rochester)
will be found at No. 80 the name "Londini;"
and again coming down the Watling Street
from Verulam (St. Albans) will be found at No.
103, "Londinium Augusta;" thereby shewing
clearly that there were two separate and distinct

towns or settlements, for it is not probable that the writer would name the same town twice. It is clear, therefore, that the Watling Street passed over a considerable portion, from Hatcham to Lambeth, of what is now Surrey, notwithstanding Ptolemy stated that Londinium belonged to the Cantii.

THE STANE STREET would appear to be the Way second in importance in the county; but it may be assumed that it is not so ancient as the Watling and some other Ways; but that it was an entirely new way made by the Romans through the great forest to shorten the distance of Chichester from London. It enters the county near Rowhook (which appears to have been a meeting or crossing place of several Ways); and proceeding very straight through Ockley to the Holmwood, near Dorking, it turns there, under Anstey-bury Camp, towards Dorking, and runs through that town to Burford Bridge, which would also, as will be seen later, appear to have been an important place of meeting and crossing of roads; and the old well-known inn there may have sheltered both Romans of old and pilgrims in mediæval times, as it does now all sorts and conditions of men.

At one time I thought this Stane Street ran over Epsom Downs to Carshalton, by a route explored by Mr. Warne ; but in consequence of some claim made a few years since for the repair of a piece of road called the Roman road, between Epsom and Walton Downs, at the back of Woodcot House, I concluded that this was in fact a continuation of the Stane Street to Epsom and Ewell, where Mr. Warne (missing the connection) professed, no doubt correctly, to find the Stane Street again ; and then it runs on in a nearly straight line by Morden, Tooting, and Balham to London.

From Rowhook, on the Stane Street just outside of Surrey, a Roman road to Farley Heath (Neomagus) was explored by Mr. J. Park Harrison ; and is fully described by him in Vol. VI. of the "Surrey Archæological Collections," with maps; I need not further allude to it ; but I may state that the "Leminge Lane," which appears close to Rowhook in the first map, would lead directly to a small square camp between Rudgwick and Alfold, which appears on the six inch Ordnance map (sheet xlvi., Surrey,) as "Broomhall Copse." This camp adjoins a road which can be traced from a round camp near

Plaistow in Sussex, past Plaistow Place, an ancient manor house of the Archbishops of Canterbury, over Gennet's Bridge, by Hook Street and Monkton Hook (a Manor Farm) and Hill House (or Moses Place), by Furzen Lane and Oakwood Hill to the Stane Street near Ockley. And I was told by an old inn-keeper at Rowhook, some forty years ago, that he had helped to take up the stones of several branches of road from that place, and one in particular running eastward towards Cradles Farm, King's Fold, Friday Street, Rome Farm, and in line to Charlewood (and a portion of this is the county boundary), so that Rowhook seems to have been an important crossing place.

THE DEVIL'S HIGHWAY is the name (just outside of the county) of a portion of a Way which runs through a corner of Surrey from Staines to Duke's Hill, Bagshot, and was surveyed and mapped by the students at Sandhurst College, in 1836, and was dignified with the name of the " Imperial Way," but upon what authority I have never been able to learn. This appears to have been a great highway from London to Bath, passing along the south side of the Kennet by Bedwin ; but the students somehow

mixed it up with the Icknield Way, and made it
cross the Kennet into the upper Bath road; and
their survey through Silchester was really of only
a branch way; for by the six inch Ordnance map
it is clear that the Devil's Highway originally ran
straight to Abel Bridge, through Wasing Park;
but when Caer Segont was made a Roman
fortress (now called Silchester), a branch was
made out of the highway, past Stratfield-Saye,
into the new fortress; and then out again, past
the Imp Stone (probably a Roman mile-stone) to
Abel Bridge; and this is what was surveyed and
mapped by the students as part of the " Imperial
Way." The Survey, which was printed in the
Gentleman's Magazine, and probably other
publications, would give the best information as
to this Way through this county.

It is by no means improbable that a branch ran
out of or crossed this Way, from Cæsar's Camp, past
the Military College, just touching this county
at Blackwater Bridge, to the great British and
Roman city of Venta Belgarum, which, I insist,
was not at Winchester, but just outside of this
county, at Ewshot, near Cæsar's Camp and
Aldershot. It may be considered as certain that
there would be a road of communication between

these two camps, and it is surprising that, with all
the railway cuttings that have been made
through the district, it has not been hit upon;
but it is probable that, not being suspected, it may
have been cut through without being noticed
by the navvies and gangers as anything
remarkable.

THE PILGRIMS' WAY requires special comment.
As regards this particular Way at least in West
Surrey, everybody wants to know, but nobody
seems to know much, about it. It appears to
have been satisfactorily traced as far westward as
Gatton; but from inquiry I have often made, of
those who I thought likely to know, as to its
course further westward, I have never been able
to obtain any more satisfactory answer than that
it ran along the slopes of the hills; but what hills
were intended by this I never could learn, nor in
fact anything more definite than such answers.

I imagine that Pilgrimages to Canterbury, and
other places, may be considered to have been
pleasant summer outings (something like our own
Archæological excursions) for parties of devout
persons, and others, who travelled together for
companionship to the places of pilgrimage; only
they did not travel in brakes and carriages, but

mostly on horseback, and some on foot ; and the
outing was not merely for a day, or two or three,
but for perhaps a fortnight or more ; and upon
the authority of Chaucer, very pleasant outings
they must have been.

Now if what is known as the " Pilgrims'
Way" from Gatton through Kent be examined,
it will be seen that it consists of a series of
ancient roads or tracks along the sides of the
hills, outside of the great forest of Andred, from
one camp to another of the ancient Britons or
Romans, in the line to and as far as Boxley
Abbey, and that the last stage is from this
Abbey to Canterbury. This gives us a clue, and
on the principle of *ex uno disce omnes*, we may
infer that what they did in this part of their
journey they would do in other parts.

Under these circumstances I must state my
conviction that this so called Way exists as a
single way not much further west than Gatton,
but that further westwards it is a series of
branches or feeders from various directions which
come to a focus in mid Surrey, say on Boxhill,
and proceeded thence to Canterbury, in the one
continuous track now bearing the name, and it
may be fairly opined that on these branches or

feeders the routes taken by the Pilgrims were, as in Kent, such of the ancient ways or tracks as happened to lead from one religious house to another, which probably were then some of the halting places or houses of entertainment on their journeys.

Mr. Leveson-Gower, in a paper read at Gatton in 1879, intimated that the Pilgrims' Way led between the two chief towns of the kingdom at that time, viz., Winchester and Canterbury, and also entered the county near Farnham. I can quite agree with both of these statements (although seemingly contradictory) if it be allowed that there were different branches or feeders of the Way used by Pilgrims coming from different parts of the country; whether from Exeter and the west, Salisbury, Winchester, Bath, or Gloucester; each would, perhaps, require a distinct branch, if, as has been suggested, they used these ancient Ways, made by the Romans from one of their stations or camps, to another station or camp, near which religious houses existed where they might find shelter and entertainment.

With this view as a basis, the only place I have ever heard of as the track of the Pilgrims'

Way in west Surrey, is in what may be called
the Tyting valley near Albury, and under St.
Martha's Hill. Therefore taking a route from
the west side of the county, where a line of the
Way is so said to have entered it, we find
Waverley Abbey, and further on Puttenham
Priory; and between these two we find the
Roman station of Hampton Lodge. We may
very well infer that there would be a military
way from Alton (Brigæ) to Hampton Lodge,
which would furnish a route for the Pilgrims;
and the ferry at St. Catherine's Hill would
furnish a direct route into the Tyting Valley,
where the Way is said to have passed along; and
thence by Weston Street up the hill on to Netley
Heath, and along the top of the hill to Dorking;
or an alternative route might be under the hill
by Shere, till it joined the branch from Winchester next described. It is probable that
Tyting was a small religious house.

Another branch, and probably the most
important, and apparently usually considered the
main line, would be from Winchester before
mentioned: but this would also take in all the
country behind it, as Cornwall, Devon, Somerset,
and Wilts; and also the foreign pilgrims arriving

at Poole and Southampton, who would come up
to Otterbourne by the well known military ways
connected with those ports, and proceed either to
Winchester, or direct to Alresford, by the way
travelled by the Emperor Hadrian, and his son-
in-law Antoninus (afterwards Emperor) as
is set out in Iter XV. of the Itinerary of
Antoninus.

I have long held a theory that from Otterbourne there was a direct line of ancient road
(probably British, but used by the Romans)
to Woolmer (Clausentum), Farley Heath
(Neomagus), and on to Carshalton and Wallington (Noviomagus); this would furnish the
Pilgrims with a line of route in the direction of
Canterbury. I do not find, however, on this
route, more than one religious house, namely
Selborne Priory, but there is evidently a continuous series of roads between old camps of
which use could be made.

Starting then from Winchester, and proceeding
to Alresford, there will be found on the map at
East Tisted, a place called " Pilgrims' Place,"
which would evidently imply the Pilgrims' route
there, and proceeding onwards to Selborne Priory,
and past the site of Clausentum, somewhere near

the Earl of Selborne's seat at Blackmore, the
route would be in line to a Roman camp called
Beacon Hill above Churt, and would enter Surrey
about Greyshot, and proceed over the top of
Hindhead, where there is a flat surface of fine
turf, now used by picnic parties, and graced by a
pillar erected by the late Justice Sir William
Erle, where I can imagine the Pilgrims of old
would make a halt, and also hold a picnic and
enjoy the splendid view from the summit.
Down the hill and outside of Witley Park,* and
by Sandal Lane, the Way would run on to
Hambledon and Hascombe, where there is a
Roman Camp on the west end of the hill, near
Park Hatch. Probably at their period, and
before it was planted with fir trees, Hascombe
Hill was covered only with heath and brushwood,
and the pilgrims could ride along the top of it,
and enjoy the prospect over the vast forest of the
Andred, at a distance of about six miles from where
I am now writing. Thence it would proceed up
Wood Hill to Farley Heath (the site of
Neomagus), and forward to Abinger and Wotton,
Westcot Street and Milton Street, with Bury

* This park was the domain of the Duke of Clarence who was
drowned in the Butt of Malmsey.

Hill and the Nower alongside, to Dorking. There is a "Nore" also on Hascomb Hill, whatever that may import. Then proceeding up Box Hill, it would probably join the military road at the top of it, and continue along it to Gatton.

Another branch of the Pilgrims' Way I can conceive would enter the county from the direction of Gloucester, Oxford, and Reading. There was doubtless a military way from Caleva (near Reading) to Pontes (Staines) through Windsor Forest, which would run in the direction of Chertsey Abbey, and consequently lead the pilgrims to take that route in their way to Canterbury; and a way would probably run through Addlestone past St. George's Camp, and on to Cobham Street and Stoke D'Abernon, and via the two Bookhams and Effingham (where I believe was an important Romano-British settlement) over the hill to Westhumble Street and Burford. The road from Burford bridge up Boxhill was always called by my father-in-law, a native of Dorking, "the military road;" we may therefore assume that the pilgrims would take this road up the hill, and at the top of it all the branches would apparently unite into one Way, and so run on over Walton Heath (where is a Roman villa) to

Gatton. Whence to Titsey at the border of the county it is sufficiently well known.

Here I may refer to another matter connected with the county. The great camp at St. George's Hill, suggests the question What could be the use of such a large inclosure? and my conviction is that it was a Camp of Refuge for the Rhemi and Bibroci, who seem, as before said, to have dwelt along the bank of the Thames, separated perhaps by the river Wey. It is remarkable how often we find large camps near the borders of adjoining tribes, as in this case; another is at Holwood Hill, between the Rhemi and the Cantæ; another at Ightham between the Cantæ and Regni; another at Cæsar's Camp, Aldershot, between the Regni and Belgæ; and still another at Cæsar's Camp near Sandhurst, between the Bibroci and Attrebatii; but the most remarkable example of a Camp of Refuge is perhaps the Pen Pits in Somerset, at the meeting of the Belgæ, Hedui, and Durotriges; where at the time of Vespasian's invasion, all the population of the east of Britain, would appear to have taken refuge, and far exceeding the limits of the camp, covered 700 acres with their huts. Cæsar seems to intimate something like this, when he describes a camp to which the Britons retreated and hid themselves, in a place fortified by nature and art, which it would appear they had already prepared, by reason of some domestic war. It is admitted that the pits at Whorlebury are hut-circles, then if so at Whorlebury, why not at Penselwood?

The following are other probable roads in East Surrey, which appears to have been the territory of the Rhemi, and being probably under direct Roman sway, consequently had more attention paid to the making of roads. The west part of Surrey was the territory of the Regni. They were probably at first merely military communications from Noviomagus to outlying camps and garrisons on the outskirts of the great forest; but some of them afterwards lengthened through the forest to the sea coast; and perhaps it will be most convenient to trace them upwards from the coast, viz. :—

A road out of Sussex, perhaps from Pevensey, by Hailsham, Maresfield, East Grinstead in Sussex, through Lingfield, Blindley Heath, Godstone, Caterham, Croydon, and Streatham to London. Streatham, it may be remarked, appears to have been a general meeting place of roads.

A road from Newhaven by Lewes, Chailey, Lingfield, and Ardingly in Sussex, by Brewer Street, Chaldon, to Wallington.

Another from Newhaven by Kingston, Plumpton to Street, and from Portslade and Patcham to Street, ran by Wivelsfield, Balcombe, and Worth, in Sussex, by Thundersfield Castle, Red Hill, Linkfield Street, Gatton, Woodmanstern, to Carshalton.

A road out of Kent from Tonbridge or Edenbridge by Limpsfield, Warlingham, and Sanderstead to Croydon.

If it be asked which of these (if either) was the south end of Erming Street, I should be inclined to say the two Ways from Newhaven and Portslade, joining near Street, and proceeding by Wivelsfield and Worth into Surrey; because these two latter places (Wivelsfield being represented by Berts, a manor in that parish) are both found in the Domesday Survey as places then known and recognized as clearances in the great forest; and Thundersfield Castle would appear to be a very evident British settlement, adopted by the Romans as a protective station of the Rhemi against the natives of the great forest.

Folk=Lore and Local Customs.

BY GEORGE CLINCH.

THE day when folk-lore was regarded as trivial and unworthy the attention of sober historians is happily past, and although it is to be regretted that the subject has not fallen to an abler pen than mine, it will not be necessary, probably, to offer any apology for devoting a few pages of this volume to those ancient superstitions of our forefathers, whose recital had the effect of closing up the circle around the cottage fireside on a winter's evening, and inspiring the rustic hearers with strange and fascinating sensations of awe.

In a county such as Surrey, possessed of an ancient civilization and strongly marked physical features, it would be remarkable if no traces of early religions and superstitions remained in place-names and local traditions.

As a matter of fact in the place-names of Surrey we have some most interesting traces of the worship formerly paid to Celtic and

7

Scandinavian deities, although almost every other indication of the cult has long since perished. Sites dedicated to the worship of Taith are indicated by such names as Toot Hill, Tooters Hill, etc., and Surrey possesses an instance of an almost identical character in Tooting. It is to be observed, however, that in this case it is not a hill, or a single site which bears evidence of the Celtic deity, but a settlement or a district inhabited by people professing that ancient faith. Of the worship of Odin, or Woden, remarkably clear evidence is afforded by such names as Woden Hill (Bagshot) and Wanborough, situated under the north slope of the Hog's Back, and possessing springs which, tradition states, have never been frozen. Wandsworth, too, derives its name from a river which was probably named after this deity. Thursley, Thundersfield, and Thunderhill, serve to remind us of the ancient Scandinavian Thor and the Anglo-Saxon form of his name, Thunor.

It is worthy of notice that three singular mounds on Frensham Common, in the vicinity of Thursley, are known as the "Devil's Jumps," and an extraordinary glen in the same neighbourhood is called the "Devil's Punchbowl." In the application of these names there is something peculiarly suggestive of the ancient Scandinavian legends of Thor's gargantuan exploits in lowering the level of the sea itself to prove the extent of his bibulous capabilities.

In many parts of the county popular tradition ascribes to Satanic influence works which do not appear at first sight capable of easy explanation. In certain cases, for instance, where an ancient church is situated at some distance from the village street, or that part of the village which is most thickly populated, a favourite explanation of the circumstance is that, whilst men proposed to build their church near their houses, the Devil, for some sinister purpose, removed their work to a distance during the night. A curious tradition lingers at Guildford relative to the building of the chapels of St. Martha and St. Catherine. Two sisters are credited with the building of these two edifices, and it is said that they were in the habit of flinging the hammer backwards and forwards to each other as they required it,

Godstone, in Surrey, like Godshill, Godstow, and similarly-named places in other counties, was probably a pagan site consecrated to Christian worship.

A writer in *The Gentleman's Magazine* of 1782, draws attention to a very curious custom which flourished about the middle of the eighteenth century at Warlingham. Early in the Spring, the boys used to go round to the several orchards in the parish, and whip the apple trees, in order to procure a plentiful crop of fruit. After that they carried a little bag to the house, where the good woman would give them some oatmeal. It was imagined that this custom had some reference to the rites anciently performed in honour of Pomona.

This reminds one of a similar custom once prevalent at Keston and West Wickham, Kent, the following particulars of which are thus recorded by the historian Hasted. In Rogation Week, about Keston and West Wickham, "a number of young men meet together, and with a hideous noise run into the orchards, and encircling each tree, pronounce these words :—

> ' Stand fast root, bear well, top,
> God send us a youling sop !
> Every twig, apple big !
> Every bough, apple enough ! '

For which incantation the confused rabble expect a gratuity in money, or drink, which is no less welcome ; but if they are disappointed of both, they with great solemnity anathematize the owners and trees with altogether as insignificant a curse. It seems highly probable that this custom has arisen from the ancient one of perambulation among the heathens, when they made prayers to the gods for the use and blessings of the fruit coming up, with thanksgiving for those of the preceding year, and as the heathens supplicated Æolus, god of the winds, for his favourable blasts, so, in this custom, they still retained his name, with a very small variation ; this ceremony is called *youling*, and the word is often used in their invocations."

The Churchwardens' Accounts at Kingston-upon-Thames contain some entries which relate to a now obsolete instrument of punishment for scolds and unquiet women. Thus, in 1572, we read that "The making of the cucking-stool" cost eight shillings. The iron-work for the same cost three shillings, the timber seven shillings and sixpence, and three brasses and three wheels cost four shillings and tenpence. The stool appears to have been in frequent use, as there are several entries of money paid for repairs.

At Walton-on-Thames another relic of barbarous times still exists, preserved in the vestry of the church. This is a "Gossip's Bridle," constructed of thin iron bands, which were intended to be passed over the head and padlocked behind the neck. In front is an aperture for the nose, and below it a tongue of iron projects inwards towards the mouth, and passing over the tongue prevents anything except a gurgling noise. This iron tongue was once two and a half inches in length, but owing to want of careful preservation it has been much corroded by rust.

It was presented to the town in 1633 by one who is said to have lost a valuable estate through a gossiping, lying woman. It bears the following halting inscription :—

> " Chester presents Walton with a bridle,
> To curb women's tongues that talk too idle."

This barbarous instrument of punishment, sometimes called a "brank," is by no means unique. Mr. Llewellynn Jewitt, in an interesting contribution to *The Reliquary* (Vol I.) on the punishment of scolds, mentions upwards of thirty examples of the brank, still preserved in various parts of the kingdom. The example at Kingston is, however, one of the earliest specimens of its kind, and although less remarkable in form than others which could be named, is very interesting on account of its dated inscription.

The celebrated case of fraud associated with the name of Mary Toft, commonly known as the "rabbet-breeder" of Godalming, illustrates in a painfully striking manner the ignorance and

PORTRAIT OF MARY TOFT.

foolish credulity of the age in which that remarkable character flourished.

During the months of November and December, 1726, this impudent imposter pretended to give birth to several rabbits. Mr. John Hunter, a surgeon of Guildford, supported this absurd story when the woman was examined, but he is supposed to have had some hand in the cheat. Mr. St. André, the King's surgeon and anatomist, Sir Richard Manningham, Dr. Douglas, Dr. Mowbray, Mr. Simborch, and several other professional men, paid some attention to this extraordinary case, and probably all were more or less taken in by the awkward deception.

For the convenience of the medical gentlemen who attended her, Mary Toft was removed from Guildford to Lacy's bagnio, in Leicester Fields, London. Suspicions of trickery seem to have been entertained by some, however, and a strict watch was kept, with the result that all was discovered. Evidence was given by the persons who had actually supplied the rabbits, and the medical authorities who at one time believed in the fraud became the laughing-stock of the neighbourhood.

A large number of satirical prints and poems were issued upon the occasion, and the whole affair seems to have made a great noise. Mary Toft was placed in custody, and subjected to an examination before Sir Thomas Clarges, but whether she received any punishment for her imposture is not known. She appears, however, to have got into trouble again later on, for in the *Weekly Miscellany*, for April 19th, 1740, we read " The celebrated Rabbit woman of Godalmin, in *Surry*, was committed to *Guildford Goal*, for receiving stolen goods."

In *The Gazetteer*, or *Daily London Advertiser*, of January 21st, 1764, we read, " Last week died at *Godalmin*, in *Surrey*, Mary *Tofts*, formerly noted for an imposition of breeding rabbits."

In the British Museum Library (1178. h. 4.) there is an interesting collection of tracts and engravings relating to the case of Mary Toft.

In the curious legends which are associated with Mother Ludlam's Cave at Moor Park, near Farnham, we have a partial survival of the belief in witchcraft which was once so general throughout the kingdom. From an account penned in 1773, or thereabout, we learn that the hole or cave " lies half way down the west side of a sandy hill, covered with wood, towards the southernmost end of Moor Park, and is near three miles south of Farnham, and about a quarter of a mile north-east of the ruins of Waverley Abbey, which were, when standing, visible from it. . . . At the entrance it is about eight feet high, and fourteen or fifteen broad, but decreases in height and breadth till it becomes so low as to be passable only by a person crawling on his hands and knees; farther on it is said to heighten. Its depth is undoubtedly considerable, but much exaggerated by the fabulous reports of the common people." The view here reproduced from an engraving after a drawing made in 1761, shows the cave with stone benches on each side, and a small stream of water running across the floor, which is paved with stone.

A popular tradition is to the effect that this subterranean cavity once formed the residence of a white witch, called Mother Ludlam, or Ludlow, who, when properly invoked, kindly assisted her poor neighbours in their necessities, by lending them such culinary utensils and household furniture as they wanted for particular occasions. Anyone who wished to borrow from the old witch used to repair to the cave at midnight, turn round three times, and thrice repeat aloud, " Pray, good Mother Ludlam, lend me such a thing (naming the utensil) and I will return it within two days." He or she then retired, and coming again early the next morning, found at

the entrance the requested article. This convenient system of borrowing is said to have
continued for a long time, until upon one occasion
a person not returning a large cauldron within
the stipulated period according to promise,
Mother Ludlam became irritated, and refused to

MOTHER LUDLAM'S CAVE.

take it back when it was afterwards left in the
cavern. From that time to this she has not
accommodated anyone with the most trifling loan.
The subsequent history of the cauldron,
according to legendary tradition, is that it was
carried to Waverley Abbey, and after the
dissolution of that house, deposited in Frensham

Church.　A large vessel of hammered copper is still preserved at that church, and is tradition- ally believed to be the very one which Mother Ludlam rejected.　Its diameter is thirty-three inches, and its depth nineteen and a half inches ; it has a large handle on each side, and rests upon a three-legged stand of wrought iron.　Nathaniel Salmon, in his *Antiquities of Surrey*, published in 1736, thus speaks of this ancient cauldron :— " The great Cauldron which lay in the Vestry beyond the Memory of Man was no more brought thither from *Waverley* than, as report goes, by the Fairies.　It need not raise any man's wonder for what use it was, there having been many in *England* till very lately to be seen, as well as very large Spits which were given for entertainment of the Parish, at the Wedding of poor Maids.　So was in some places a Sum of Money charged upon Lands for them ; and a House for them to dwell in for a year after Marriage."

The accompanying illustration has been prepared from a photograph taken by Mr. George E. Langrish, who has also kindly supplied dimensions of this quaint old relic of bygone times at Frensham.

The tract of country lying between Holmwood Common and Reigate, is supposed to have been occupied by those ancient Britons whom the Romans were unable to drive out. It afforded a similar retreat to the Saxons when the Danes ravaged the country in all directions. The following proverbial distich is attributed to the

CAULDRON AT FRENSHAM CHURCH.

inhabitants of the neighbourhood, in connection with these circumstances, by Camden :—

"The Vale of Holmesdale,
   Never wonne, ne never shall."

The locality derives it name from the abundance of holm oak which grows there, and among which red deer flourished until a late date. In the days of the Duke of York, who afterwards became James II., some of the largest stags ever seen in England were hunted in this district

Hydon Ball, or Highdown Ball as it is sometimes written, the highest point of a range of hills to the south of Godalming, overlooking the wealds of Surrey and Sussex, has a curious old rhyme associated with it, to the following effect :—

> "On Hydon's top there is a cup,
>   And in that cup there is a drop,
>   Take up the cup and drink the drop,
>   And place the cup on Hydon's top."

The exact meaning of the mystic ceremony here alluded to is perhaps for ever lost, but it seems not improbable that it had some reference to a religious rite, and probably it is of great antiquity.

The mock ceremony of electing a Mayor of Garrett upon the meeting of every new Parliament was once kept up with considerable spirit, but it died out before the end of the last century, the last election taking place in 1796. Foote's farce, entitled "The Mayor of Garret," published in 1764, probably had a good deal to do with attracting popular attention to this absurd custom, which took place at what was then a small hamlet situated between Wandsworth and Tooting. Brayley tells us the candidates were generally half idiotic and deformed persons, who were induced to accept the office by the

SIR JEFFREY DUNSTAN.

persuasion of the publicans. The latter provided gay clothing as an attraction, with a view, no doubt, to making a considerable profit out of the custom which the day's frolic would be sure to bring to their houses.

Two of the most celebrated mayors were Sir Jeffrey Dunstan, a hawker of old wigs, and Sir Harry Dimsdale, a muffin-crier.

The tolling of the "pancake bell" was kept up at Dorking every Shrove Tuesday until a recent period, and as late as the year 1862, if not more recently, the day was observed by many ancient customs. First the streets were perambulated by the football retinue, composed of grotesquely-dressed persons, to the sounds of music, and the afternoon was devoted to the kicking of the ball up and down the chief streets. The play was often rough, and sometimes, as the afternoon advanced, even dangerous to the limbs of the competitors.

Palm Sunday was formerly an important day at Crowhurst. From time immemorial a fair or wake was held on that day in the churchyard, liquors were sold, and excesses frequently committed.

Another curious custom, and one which bears the mark of extreme antiquity, was the annual pilgrimage of all youths, maidens, old folks, and children, to St. Martha's Hill on Good Friday. Music and dancing were the chief amusements in which the pilgrims indulged, and the meaning of the festival is involved in great obscurity, but it is not improbable that it is some kind of survival of an early religious ceremony. It clearly has no reference to the solemn event celebrated upon Good Friday by Christians.

Michælmas Eve, or the Sunday evening which preceded it, was called at Kingston-on-Thames, "Crack·Nut Sunday," from the curious custom

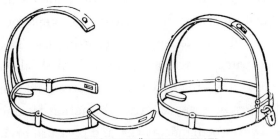

THE "SCOLD'S BRIDLE," WALTON-ON-THAMES.

which prevailed among the congregation of cracking nuts during the service in the church. It has been thought probable that this custom may have originated from the usual civic feast attending the choosing of the bailiff and other members of the corporate body on Michælmas Day.

Southwark in the Olden Time.

By Mrs. Edmund Boger.

WHEN, more than half a century before the Christian Era, Julius Cæsar led his legions from Deal, by some route answering to the Old or New Kent Road, he kept on the Surrey side of the river, not crossing the Thames till he came to Coway Stakes, near Walton-on-Thames. His road lay through forest and morass, and so gradual was the transformation from forest scenery to woodlands, parks, and pleasure grounds, and thence to mazes of bricks and mortar, dismal alleys and densely populated courts, that only sixty years since, cows grazed within a hundred yards of the river between Southwark and Blackfriars Bridge Roads.

Ptolemy, the Geographer, in the second century avers that London was originally built on the south side of the river, but this seems scarcely probable, the mistake, however, if such it is, shows at least the importance of Southwark at that early date. Boadicea's fierce onslaught on the

Romans seems to have led to its first material improvement, those who escaped the massacre fled over the river, and with the Romans always came progress and civilization. Possibly it was then that the river was embanked, and Bankside, so famous a name in English literature, first formed.

Memorials of the Roman occupation in the shape of brass rings, pottery and coins, sepulchral urns and tesseræ have been found close to London Bridge, in the precincts of St. Saviour's, which, as we are writing of the olden time, will henceforth be called by its ancient name of St. Mary Overie. The name Overie is of course of the same origin as Surrey ; it signifies over the river, but Bartholomew Linstead, the last Prior, told a tale of how the Priory was built by Mary Awdry as a religious house for Sisters. This story of Linstead's becoming somehow connected with the stone figure of a skeleton in the North Transept (a not uncommon *memento mori* monument), an absurd legend was devised of the death of an old miser to whom the Ferry belonged, and the dedication of his hoards by his only daughter, Mary, to the founding of a house for Sisters, of which she herself, absurdly enough, became the Patron Saint !

However originally founded, a religious house there was, close to Bankside and London Bridge, in the days of Saint Swithin, Bishop of Winchester, 852-862 (in these days more esteemed for his supposed influence on the weather in July and August, than for his saintliness and manifold good works), he changed the house of Sisters into a college of priests. So early was the intimate connection between the Bishops of Winchester and Southwark, a connection which lasted more than a thousand years! This College of Priests appears to have erected a wooden bridge over the river, and a toll was probably paid for its use, as well as the Ferry.

When the kings of Wessex became kings of England, the traffic would be naturally increased over the one connecting link between the opposite sides of the river.

On the north and south-east ends respectively of London Bridge, are the churches of St. Olave and St. Magnus, father and son, both Kings of Norway. St. Olave's belongs to Southwark, both locally and historically. In 994 Olave, or Olaus, who had accompanied Sweyn, King of Denmark, in a raid upon England, fell under good influence, he embraced the Christian faith and was baptized.

In 1014 we find him again in England, but this time assisting Ethelréd the Unréd * against his former allies.   London was captured by the Danes, he assisted Ethelred to retake it, breaking down the Bridge by some contrivance of beams and chains, and a great number of the enemy were drowned.

In 1016 Canute's fleet sailed up the Thames, but some obstacle, probably the remains of the old Bridge and Olave's rude engines, round which other debris would collect, prevented his passage, and Canute was compelled to dig a canal on the south side before he could place his ships on the western end.   The good work that Olave did for England was not forgotten, and, appropriately enough, after his martyrdom by his heathen subjects, a church was built on the very spot where he had so valiantly assisted the English against their foes.

Southwark has always delighted in processions, the first was also unique ; it was the translation of the body of Saint Alphege from its temporary resting place in St. Paul's, to Canterbury.   The Archbishop had been taken prisoner by the Danes in 1011, and finding that he refused to be

* Nay, not wise counsel, but want of counsel.

ransomed by his impoverished diocese, they brought him out at a feast they were holding at Greenwich. "Gold, Bishop, give us gold," they shouted, but he stedfastly refused; then, pelted with bones of oxen and other missiles, he fell down, and his sufferings were ended by a blow from the axe of a man he had lately baptized. His body was yielded to the Bishops of London and Dorchester. Twenty-one years afterwards, Canterbury demanded the body of their murdered Archbishop. It was granted, and Canute himself steered the barge on which it was conveyed from St. Paul's to Southwark. Here he was received by a stately procession, consisting of his successor, with his Suffragans and attendant clergy. "With a worshipful band and sprightly joy they conveyed him to Rochester. Here came Emma the Lady * and her young son Hardacanute, and they all with much state and songs of praise bore the Holy Archbishop into Canterbury." †

It is the year 1052, in what we call the peaceful days of the Confessor; yet, strange to say, an entirely unique and warlike pageant was witnessed from Bankside. Two hostile fleets lay within

---

* Widow of Ethelred, and wife of Canute.
† The 19th of April in our calendar is dedicated to St. Alphege.

a short distance of each other in the Thames.
Earl Godwin had returned from banishment, and
was with his fleet off Southwark, where he had a
palace ; but, says the Saxon Chronicle, "his
band continually diminished the longer he stayed."
It was probably this fact that made him listen to
overtures of peace. King Edward's fleet of fifty
vessels was on the opposite side nearer Westminster. So peace was made, for the armies
would not fight "English against English," and
"great folly it was that they should join battle,
because all that was most noble in England was
in the two armies."

In 1066 when three kings reigned and two
battles were fought on English soil, our Borough
was the scene of much that went on, when Harold
posted northwards to oppose his brother Tosti
and the King of Norway, and then returned
flushed with victory, to defeat and death at
Hastings. Southwark was given to the flames
by the advanced guard of the conqueror's army.
St. Mary Overie was either burned in the fire,
or destroyed by a hurricane which swept away
London Bridge in 1091.

And now began the work of restoration.
Alwyn Childe, a Saxon merchant, led the way ;

he built or rebuilt the Abbey of St. Saviour's at Bermondsey. The name of Bermondsey is probably derived from that of some Saxon noble, and the termination ey or eyot stands for island, and in times not long past, Bermondsey was a land of eyots, of unsavoury ditches, of bridges, etc. St. Saviour's was an abbey complete in all its parts, it had large possessions granted at different periods by kings, queens, and other benefactors, and several of the bishops and abbots who came to London to attend Parliament or Convocation, had houses here which they rented from the Abbot of Bermondsey. In many cases the name still remains. A Rochester house is still near London Bridge. Battle Stairs shows where the Abbot of Battle took to his barge; close by were houses belonging to the Abbots of Lewes, St. Augustine's, Canterbury, and Hyde. One can almost trace the boundaries of Bermondsey Abbey by the names of the streets. Grange Road marks the farm buildings. Pickle Herring Street the place where the monks cured the fish against fasting days. One Alan Perrot gave an acre of land and 6000 herrings to the Abbey. Does this queerly named street represent Alan Perrot's

acre? Bermondsey Square occupies the site of
the principle quadrangle. Abbey Street marks
the position of the Great Church, while Long-
walk is said to show its exact length. St.
Saviour's Dock near Tooley Street, once belonged
to Bermondsey Abbey, while St. Mary Overie's
Dock still remains close to what was St. Mary
Overie's Church.* The quaint conservatism of
their names shows how all else has changed.

The chief glory of St. Saviour's, Bermondsey,
was its wonder-working rood, to which pilgrimages were made down to the time of the
Reformation. It was brought, so the legend
says, to England by St. Augustine, and it or another (for there were several roods at Bermondsey,
in fact I think it likely that they were used as
boundary stones) was afterwards fished out of the
Thames. Crucifix Lane is said to be the place
where Sir Thomas Pope, himself a Romanist, set
up the Rood after the destruction of the Abbey
by Henry VIII. How Sir Thomas Pope recon-
ciled his traffic in holy things with his principles,

---

* So completely has Bermondsey Abbey passed out of mind, that
Knight in his history of London adduces a story of one Joan Baker,
who in 1510, expressed her regret at having gone on pilgrimages to
St. Saviour's, as showing that St. Mary Overie had already changed its
name before the Reformation. St. Saviour's was St. Saviour's of
Bermondsey. Pilgrimages were not made to St. Mary Overie.

one does not quite see, possibly Trinity College, Oxford, was founded as an atonement.

On St. Matthias's day in the year 1558 did the Bishop of Rochester preach at Paul's Cross, and the Rood of " St. Saviour's, Bermondsey, was taken down."

To return to earlier times, it is curious to note what a favourite abode of female Royalty this Abbey was in the middle ages. Here Mary of Scotland, wife to the Count of Boulogne, died. Her daughter Maude was probably here educated, Catherine of France, widow of Henry V., mother of Henry VI., and, through her second marriage, with Owen Tudor, grandmother to Henry VII., also died here, and here in poverty and neglect died Elizabeth Woodville, Queen of Edward IV., and mother of Henry VII.'s Queen, Elizabeth of York.

In the first year of Henry I., William Gifford, Chancellor, was appointed Bishop of Winchester. He recognized at once the importance of South-wark as the connecting link between Winchester, the capital of England, and the great port of London, and built a palace on Bankside. He formed a park with stately trees, terraces, fish-ponds, etc. Park Street, which runs parallel to

Bankside, keeps this in mind, and two at least of the trees in the Bishop of Winchester's Park remain in Messrs. Potts, Vinegar Yard, in Summer Street, which was called after a late bishop of Winchester.

Two crusading knights now appear on the scene, William de Pont de L'Arche * and William Dauncy; in connection with Bishop Gifford they rebuilt St. Mary Overie on its present lines : it was a fine cruciform church, with a central tower, and the architecture of the choir shows exactly the point where the massive Norman was passing into the graceful early English, it possesses much of the peculiar beauties of both. Two priors' tombs are in the north wall of the Choir Aisle. On one of these is placed a fine wooden figure of a cross-legged knight, which was discovered lying neglected in the Church. One would fain believe it represents one of the two founders, but experts say it is of later date, and prefer rather to assign it to one of the lords of Warrenne and Surrey, who were lords of Southwark. It may be so, but Robert of Normandy's tomb in Gloucester Cathedral has a wooden figure of the Duke upon

* Sir W. de Pont de L'Arche was treasurer to Henry I., and as the royal treasuries were still kept at Winchester, he would naturally be in constant communication with the Bishop.

it, which would be of the same date as the effigy
of one of these knights.

True to his name, Sir William de Pont de
L'Arche materially assisted also in the ·rebuilding
of London Bridge. Successive Bishops of
Winchester vied with each other in restoring
and beautifying the ancient church, which in
truth served them as a town cathedral. Peter
des Roches, Cardinal Beaufort, Bishop Fox,
and Gower the poet, were among its benefactors.
In olden times it possessed three chapels, the
eastern one was, in later times, called the
Bishop's Chapel, from its containing the tomb
of Bishop Andrews, but it must have been,
one would suppose, the original Lady Chapel;
what is *now* called the Lady Chapel being
in fact the retro-choir. Another chapel was
that of St. John the Baptist, in which Gower
was originally buried; the third, that of St.
Mary Magdalene, was the Parish Church. When
the chapels were destroyed, the tombs of Gower
and Bishop Andrews were removed into the
church.

Both St. Saviour's, Bermondsey, and the Priory
of St. Mary Overie had schools attached to them :
the first, Stow affirms to be the one mentioned

by Fitz-Stephen in the time of Henry II. as with that of St Paul's and Westminster Abbey being the three principal schools in London. Both St. Saviour's and St. Mary Overie's schools were swept away at the destruction of the monasteries. St. Mary's Church was saved by Gardiner, Bishop of Winchester, who assisted the inhabitants to buy it and make it the Parish Church; in consequence of which the parishioners were their own rector and the chaplains merely their nominees. This objectionable system has now happily been amended. Southwark, however, had taken a Puritan twist, and the name of St. Mary Overie was voted Popish, and exchanged for that of St. Saviour, Bermondsey Abbey having disappeared. The School was restored and endowed by the parishioners. Shortly afterwards St. Olave's followed its example; the two schools remain to the present day.

A pillar in the south transept has upon it a cardinal's hat beneath the Beaufort arms. Of all the grand ecclesiastical functions performed in this church, none is more interesting than the marriage of James I. of Scotland, the Poet King, to Joan Beaufort, niece of the Cardinal. The wedding feast was held at Winchester House.

The bridge built by William de Pont de L'Arche was burned in 1136. It was rebuilt in 1176, one Peter of Colechurch, grand master of the Freemasons, being the architect. In the interval Becket's murder had taken place, and a chapel on the centre pier of the east side of the new bridge was a principal feature, it was dedicated to the lately-made saint and martyr. Peter himself was here buried. The last journey Becket ever took had been to Winchester House, to confer with the aged Bishop of Winchester, Henry of Blois, who in his day had been as great a stickler for the church's privileges as himself. A mandate from "the young king," Henry II.'s eldest son, made him turn for the last time from " the city of his birth to that of his death."

In 1212, St. Mary Overie being burned down, the canons erected a temporary lodging on the other side of the way, but when they were able to return to their home, the hostel or hospitium was found so convenient for the reception of the retainers of their many visitors, and as an infirmary for the sick, that, dedicating it to the memory of St. Thomas á Becket, they retained it. Robert the abbot or prior of Bermondsey erected in 1216 a house close adjoining for the use "conversorum* et puerorum," which also was dedicated in the name of St. Thomas á Becket. This was called the Eleemosynary or Almonry. † These two similar foundations were incorporated by Peter des Roches, and called " the Spital of St. Thomas the Martyr of Canterbury." St. Thomas's Hospital served many more purposes than we now understand the name to imply ; much of both useful and ornamental art work was here carried on.   In 1527 the contract for the painted windows of King's College, Cambridge, was sign- ed by James Nycolson of St. Thomas's Spyttel in Southwark ; and ten years later the first entire English bible printed in England is inscribed " Imprynted in Southwark, in St. Thomas's Hospital, by James Nycolson."

In spite of all its varied good works, the Spital of St. Thomas shared the fate of the monasteries.   It was restored to somewhat of its former use by Edward VI., after Ridley's famous sermon, but the name must be altered, for had not Becket's tomb been destroyed at Canterbury, and his name erased from our prayer book ?   Trinity

---

* Converts from the world, *i.e.*, monks ?

† The name after the manner of Southwark names was corrupted into Armoury.   The site is now occupied by the printing establishment of Messrs. M'Corquodale, St. Thomas's Street.

Hospital, and King's, in compliment to Edward, were tried, but the people did not take kindly to them, so by an odd compromise it was decided to call it still St. Thomas's, but it was to be St. Thomas the Apostle and *not* St. Thomas of Canterbury.

And now to speak of inns, of which Southwark possessed a goodly number. Stowe enumerates the Spurre, the Christopher, Bull, Queene's Head, Kinge's Head, Tabarde, George, and White Harte. The last three retained thirty years ago somewhat of their ancient appearance, being built round three sides of a square courtyard, with galleries above, into which the doors and windows of the rooms opened. Inns served in olden times not only as hotels, but were the clubs, the music halls, the concert rooms, and the theatres of the middle ages. A mere fragment of the George Inn is now all that is left.

The White Harte has been immortalized by both Shakespeare and Dickens. The Tabard, the most interesting of all, might have been spared; it represented, if not the birth, at least the coming of age of English literature. As a national memorial it might have ranked with Shakespeare's birth-place, for there it was that Chaucer from its

gallery watched the arrival of that typical band
of pilgrims he has so marvellously pourtrayed.

It was in April, 1383, that mine host of the
Tabard, Harry Bailly by name, had given notice
that a party of pilgrims would set out from his
inn.   He is well described by Chaucer, yet strange
to say we know more of him than Chaucer tells
us.   One Henry Fitz-Martin, in the reign of
Henry III., was by letters patent constituted
Bailiff of Southwark, and Harry Bailly was almost
certainly his descendant; but it is *quite* certain that
he twice represented the Borough in Parliament;
in the fiftieth year of Edward III., 1376, at Westminster, and in 1378, the second year of Richard
II., at Gloucester.   The Tabard Inn had something of an ecclesiastical character.   An Abbot
of Hyde bought the site in 1306.   He built the
inn, and had a residence for himself within it;
in 1307 he had a license from the Bishop of
Winchester for a chapel at his hospitium.

It is not too much to say that the three
greatest achievements in English literature, the
works of Chaucer and of Shakespeare, together
with the unfettered spread of the English Bible,
are inseparably connected with Southwark.

It is difficult in the work-a-day and sordid

9

surroundings of Southwark now, to realize the times when there were elements of colour and magnificence, which have now wholly disappeared.

Such a procession as the entrance of the Prince and Princess of Wales, in 1863, into London, had certainly not been seen since the restoration of Charles II., but was in the middle ages of constant occurrence. During the brilliant days of Edward III., armies with all the pomp and circumstance of war were constantly passing and re-passing through Southwark over London Bridge into the city, which then formed one continuous street, as there were houses on both sides of the bridge. Best known of all, perhaps, is the Black Prince's return from Poictiers when, in his proud humility, he rode on a small palfrey as attendant on his captive, King John of France, who was mounted on a magnificent cream-coloured charger.

Three times did Henry V. pass through our street in great state on his return from France, once on his return from Agincourt, with his train of royal and princely captives. Again after the treaty of Troyes, when he brought with him his beautiful but insipid bride, Katherine of France, and for the last time when the victor-lord was laid low in death, attended, as chief mourner, by his captive friend James I., King of Scotland.

In 1555 the Lady Chapel of St. Mary Overie was desecrated by the condemnation of the Protestant Martyrs after their so-called trial by Bishop Gardiner.

Leaving these recollections, we must hasten to the period when literature reached its highest development, and became connected with Bankside.

It was in 1586 that William Shakespeare, barely two-and-twenty, but already the father of three children, was driven from his home at Stratford-upon-Avon, to try his fortune in Southwark. He was thrown at once into that motley group of actors and authors that congregated on Bankside. The Falcon Inn,* said to have been the largest in Surrey, witnessed many of the wit combats between Ben Jonson and Shakespeare ; Sir Walter Raleigh, a member of the Mermaid Club was there too.   Beaumont and Fletcher those twin authors whose house was on the bank, here planned out their plots.   In Elizabeth's reign England is said to have been a nest of singing birds, and on Bankside many of them tried

---

* The site, for years occupied by Astley Pellat's glassworks, is now the factory for Epps's cocoa.

their notes and pruned their wings for flight. Over all towered the mighty genius of Shakespeare, he was preserved, by his home affections and his unremitting industry, from the failures and despair of others. Green, his relation, died miserably in a wretched lodging. Marlowe, the finest dramatic author before his time, perished in a tavern brawl. Massinger was found dead in his bed on Bankside. The theatres with which Shakespeare's name are associated were the Rose, the Hope, the Swan, and above all the Globe. Of these the Rose alone now leaves its name in Rose Alley. The White Bear public house, close by, is said to mark the spot where Shakespeare lived. The Swan was larger than the others, and was nearer Paris Gardens and Blackfriars.

It has been noticed that exquisite as Shakespeare's fancy was, marvellous his delineation of character, extraordinary as were the wisdom of his words which have become with us proverbial sayings, yet, in originality of plot he was wholly deficient, so that with one exception all his plays can be traced to earlier ones or old romances. A curious exemplification of this is his character of Prince Henry, afterwards Henry V. The description of his follies is known to have been grossly exaggerated ; his life having been remarkably pure and stainless ; one only escapade of his which would give the smallest foundation for his character as Madcap Harry, was his robbing the royal mails, when he could in no other way get the arrears of the income which belonged to him as Prince of Wales. The fact is, that at the very time when Shakespeare was living in Southwark, one John Popham, a barrister by profession, was performing the very same wild pranks, associating with the same dissolute companions as he represents Prince Henry to have done. The tears of his wife, and the birth of a son, are said to have worked a reformation, he parted with his boon companions in the same way that Shakespeare represents the Prince doing, and became in due course Sir John Popham, and Lord Chief Justice of England. This coincidence has, as far as I know, not before been noticed, but it can be substantiated by reference to Lord Campbell's " Lives of the Chief Justices."

When Beaumont married, Fletcher still continued to live on Bankside, he was buried at St. Saviour's, as also was " Philip Massinger," " a stranger," Edmund Shakespeare, a brother of the poet, and Laurence Fletcher, an actor.

Besides the theatres were enclosures for bull and bear baiting, and Queen Elizabeth visited Bankside, with the French Ambassador, to see what Evelyn a hundred years later called " this rude and dirty pastime." Plays were performed at court as they have been lately before our own Queen. Edward Alleyne, keeper of the King's Bears on Bankside, was the founder of the college of " God's gift " at Dulwich, and other charities.

Four bishops of Winchester have found at St. Saviour's their last resting-place. Sandall 1319, Horne 1581, William Wickham * (*not* William of Wykeham) who only lived nine months after he was translated from Lincoln—a stone in the church-yard which formerly had a brass, nearly opposite the door into the south aisle of the choir, is pointed out as marking his burial place; but the most notable is Launcelot Andrews, one of the original translators of the bible; he was the last Bishop of Winchester who lived on Bankside.

In the possession of the Marquis of Salisbury at Hatfield, is a picture—erroneously said to represent Henry VIII. and Anne Boleyn at a country wake or fair. This, however, is a mistake,

---

* He was one of five bishops who married the five daughters of Barlow, Bishop of Bath and Wells, the first married bishop after the Reformation.

the spot is Horslydown in Bermondsey, as its
situation, with regard to the Tower of London
and the Thames, shows.   The sports going on of
archery and hawking—the local magnates parad-
ing in front, the local accessories, costumes, etc.,
make it a most interesting scene.   At the right
hand corner are two figures, which may well
represent Ben Jonson and William Shakespeare,
" taking notes."

The manor of Paris Gardens, near Blackfriars,
once belonged to one Robert of Paris, and in the
middle ages was a favourite resort for the citizens
of London, who came over the river in wherries
or boats in the evening for air and relaxation.
Between these and the Bishop of Winchester's
Park, was a place of ill-repute, where the trees
stood so thick that they screened malefactors who
had fled from the city, and the place was render-
ed still more unsavoury by an order in the time
of Richard II. that the garbage and refuse from
the butchers' shambles should be thrown here,
into the ditches which had been cut to drain away
the water when a rise of the Thames threatened to
overflow the lands of Southwark and Bermondsey.

There could be much found to say on the

prisons of Southwark, especially the Marshalsea, so connected with Dickens both in fact and fiction. St. Thomas Waterings would have many a ghastly tale to tell. Penry—author of the "Marprelate Tracts"—was here executed with circumstances of great brutality. Others there were, connected more or less with Southwark, men famous or infamous in their time, whose names one can barely mention, Bishop Bonner and Robert Brown, Bunyan and Abraham Newlands, Sir Christopher Wren and Dr. Sacheverell, etc., etc.

John Harvard, was the son of a butcher, who, however, was a man of substance and position. He was one of the governors of St. Saviour's School, and it is more than probable therefore that his son John was educated there. Thence he proceeded to Emmanuel College, Cambridge. Having imbibed Puritan ideas he started for the new world in 1637, became interested in a foundation for "the Education of English and Indian youth in Knowledge and in Godliness," and died in the following year of consumption; bequeathing his library and half his property to it. In memory of him it is called Harvard College,*

* The writer had the pleasure of taking Mr. Justin Winsor, the librarian of Harvard, over St. Saviour's Church.

and the township of Newtown became Cambridge, Massachussets. Again we find literature connected with Southwark, but this time she is handing on the torch to another hemisphere, to a new world.

Hogarth's picture of Southwark Fair must close the account of Bygone Southwark. A quaint description of it in verse in Dr. Tussler's book, " Hogarth Moralized," is too long to be inserted here. After existing for several hundred years the fair was put an end to for the odd reason that " a dreadful earthquake in Jamaica was profanely and ludicrously represented in a puppet play, or some such lewd pastime." Probably the fair had become a nuisance, and this excuse was as good as any other.

" Southwark in the olden time," is our subject, yet before drawing this sketch to an end, one picture must be attempted of the present day, more gorgeous than any scene in the olden time. It is true that most of the interest of Bankside lies in the past; yet it lives not alone in its memories, but has a present beauty and glory all its own. Only let any lover of the picturesque and magnificent in art and nature go down to Bank-

side on a fine summer evening, when the sounds
of labour are hushed, and the barges are gliding
slowly past, or laid up for the night.   The sun as
it sinks in the west blazes with a gorgeous crimson light; smoky bands of vapour cross the fiery
ball; again it shines out in golden or crimson
splendour, and sends long streams of glittering
sheen across the water.   The barges, freshly
painted for the summer in green and red, catch
the light, and the rich brown sails stand out against
the glittering sky; while small boats shoot across
the shining track.   St. Paul's on the opposite
shore stands out with a strange brightness
against the northern sky, as though it were cut
out in ivory, and under the arches of the western
bridges the river seems on fire.

Mediæval Croydon.

By S. W. Kershaw, f.s.a.

THE rapid growth of most of our towns can chiefly be traced to the agencies and institutions of the middle ages. The long and wasting wars of the Roses, which had plunged England into distress, were subsiding—there was a new spirit abroad, one of increased security and comfort, and also of commercial enterprise. Under these conditions, architecture and the allied arts came into great prominence, the erection of churches was followed by the further development of domestic buildings—the houses of the nobles were rising in all their stately splendour, while schools of learning were established by royal and pious founders.

More or less, this influence was felt in our towns—some were better adapted than others for this progressive action—the cathedral cities naturally had resources denied to smaller centres, but each and all, from the grim and fortified border town, to the humble village with its thatched or timbered cottage, spoke of the extending movements of the age.

This development was reached to a certain extent in Elizabeth's days, when comfort and refinement was shown in the altered conditions of life.

The gloomy fortress of the eleventh and twelfth century gave place to the graceful Tudor mansion. Brick and stone were freely used in building, and ornament, both in carved wood and graceful iron work, was asserting its sway.

Fantastic gables and gilded turrets rose to break the monotonous line of many an ancient manor house, and deftly interwoven in the angle or balustrade were the initials or device of the owner, sometimes hidden under a strange motto or punning rebus on his name.

Croydon, the border town of the great Surrey and Kentish Weald, which stretched from near Ashford in one county, to Reigate in the other, claims peculiar interest on account of its long-worn chronicle of church and state.

In Domesday, we read Archbishop Lanfranc held Croydon. The manor, except during two periods, has been successively in the possession of the See of Canterbury, and for some five centuries the Primates have made Croydon more or less their residence, identifying their name with the parish church and its annals, with several documents signed from this manor or dwelling house, and by historical events which have transpired during the occupancy of their ancient Surrey home. One can only touch on the remote annals of the town—its position near the great Roman roads, and the remains of villas and coins in the immediate neighbourhood, all of which indicate its ancient origin.

We are, however, concerned with the far later period of the fifteenth and sixteenth centuries, when one saw better developed those buildings and their general features, which specially characterised mediæval times.

Situated on the border of the great North wood (Norwood) which bounded it Londonwards, having to the south the rising Downs, and the distant Wealden forests, Croydon naturally afforded an advantageous site, ere the metropolis was reached. The central point of local interest, and even of human, seems to have clustered round the parish church, and that was pre-eminently the case here. For after the early building, mentioned in Domesday, was destroyed, a larger structure arose, which had for its master-builders Stafford and Chichele, Archbishops of Canterbury, the latter of whom is associated with the foundation of All Souls', Oxford, with the erection of the so-called Lollard's Tower at Lambeth Palace, and received his education at the famous Winchester College, founded by William of Wykeham.

The thirteenth and fourteenth centuries were a great building age, and some of the fairest of our minsters and churches are an evidence of this wide development, for the lofty towers, the grand western windows, the canopied shrines, or sculptured chantries, displayed the skill of the artist, and the munificence of the donor.　Founded by Archbishop Courtenay, the old parish church partook of a somewhat mixed character, from the early Gothic to the late Perpendicular, and in its onward progress enshrined around it the life work of more than one of the Primates of the ancient See of Canterbury.　Of the former structure, little remains but the tower and the outer walls, for a destructive fire in 1867 reduced the rest to a ruin,* and nearly all the fine monuments perished in the flames.　In the

---

* A fine mural painting of St. Christopher also perished in the fire.

memorials to Archbishops Grindal, Whitgift, and Sheldon, one saw illustrated that phase of monumental art, which, though of late design, is such a feature of many church interiors, and a very biography in stone or marble of the illustrious past.

An exact re-production of the effigy to Whitgift, executed in 1888, enables the mediæval student to picture the original, rich in colour, ornament, and heraldic device, of the founder of Whitgift Hospital, which we shall presently notice. In this church many consecrations occurred in early times, and among the long list of divines may be singled out the names of Miles Coverdale, Bishop of Exeter, the translator into English of the first printed Bible, and of John Scory, Bishop of Rochester, who assisted at the consecration of Matthew Parker, in Lambeth Palace Chapel, in 1559. From the old church, some of the brasses, fragments of mouldings, carved brackets, and other relics, have been saved, and these, with the registers, dating from 1538, makes it indeed a storehouse of ecclesiastical lore. From the churchyard, the mellowed brick walls of the old palace look down upon us, and, as we enter the building through a small doorway, we are hardly prepared for a long historical gossip with people and scenes which have helped to make up the annals of England.

"I love this old house, and am very desirous of amusing myself, if I could find means to do it, with a history of the building." So wrote Archbishop Herring to Dr. Ducarel in 1754, about this place, then called "Croydon House," in those days, and long before, a favourite retreat of the Archbishops.

The manor house of Croydon, like the church, dates from an early period, even so far ago as 1273 ; and on this, their country abode, some of the architect-Primates bestowed much loving care and skill, as the several coats of arms now remaining in the great hall testify. The representation of coat armour on building was much in use at this time, and served to preserve the remembrance of different benefactors.

Chief among these were Archbishops Chichele, Arundel, Stafford, Bourchier and Cranmer, and even after the Commonwealth, additions and improvements were made by successive occupants.

The apartments have been much altered since the days when royalty came with trains of nobles, and sagacious statesmen discussed the intricacies of government and national policy. The Great Hall, in which many a courtly pageant was held, still retains its fine open timber roof, somewhat like that of Christ Church, Oxford, and there is happily enough of the building left to realize vividly the visit of Queen Elizabeth, in

THE GREAT HALL, CROYDON PALACE.

1573, to Archbishop Parker, her valued friend, and once chaplain to her mother, Ann Boleyn. In 1574, the Primate again entertained his sovereign with splendour, and among that brilliant group of courtiers were, Cecil, Lord Burleigh, the Earl of

Leicester, and Secretary Walsingham, names long chronicled in English annals. Archbishop Cranmer was at Croydon, when he was summoned to attend Henry VIII. at his palace at Westminster, but ere he could arrive the king was speechless, having previously uttered the memorable words, " I will see no one but Cranmer, and not him yet." The aged Prelate Grindal, after the resignation of his See, lived much here, and one can but sympathize with him in the harsh treatment he received from the Queen, on the

AUTOGRAPH OF ARCHBISHOP CRANMER.

subject of the " Prophesyings," and the loss of a faithful friend and servant.

All the rooms of " Croydon House" have had their varying historical interest, and in the chapel we are carried back in thought to early times, for ordinations and consecrations have taken place here for nearly 400 years, and the interior, though greatly altered, still retains many traces of the past. The carved bench ends and panellings point to the period of Laud and Juxon, the latter of whom, after the spoliation of the chapel during the Commonwealth, sought to repair with due care so historic a fabric. An ornamented upper pew, rich in Tudoresque carvings, is said to have been that which Queen Elizabeth used when a visitor here, and was approached from the private rooms of the palace. The "Long Gallery," that indispensable adjunct to mediæval houses, was greatly altered and re-built by Archbishop Wake; in 1587, we read that, when Sir Christopher Hatton was appointed Lord Chancellor, the Great Seal was delivered him here. These galleries have, from their situation, often been the scene of stately incident or homely gossip, serving, from their situation, as a kind of antechamber to the more private apartments, or to the larger gatherings in the Hall. A somewhat smaller chamber at Croydon was the "Guard Room," probably built by Archbishop Arundel from his arms appearing prominently therein. Round and outside this house were the gardens, and what was very noticeable the Vineyard. In old times grapes were much more cultivated than now, and in the reign of Edward III. wine was, by statute, to be tried twice a year, at Easter and at Michaelmas.

Ducarel * says "that the Church of Canterbury was plentifully furnished with vines at St. Martin's, Chartham, and Hollingbourne, in Kent," at the period above mentioned. A large moat and fish ponds, fed by the limpid streams of the Wandle, surrounded the house, and the neighbouring woods were once so thick as to

THE GATEWAY, CROYDON PALACE.

attract the notice of Lord Chancellor Bacon when riding in that direction. Gone are all these fair surroundings, even the archway, which once formed part of the gateway lodge, a former approach to this house. The keeper of this manor house enjoyed his office by patent from the

* "History of Croydon Palace."

Archbishop, and a long succession of these worthy guardians appears for more than two hundred years. Those buildings which are left have a picturesque charm in strong contrast to the modern streets and houses. Should we not then proclaim aloud the words of a modern writer, " It becomes a kind of social duty to preserve such wreckage of old things as the tempest of change has left, any relics that they find still mouldering in the flotsam and jetsam of time."*

It is not in the buildings only, but in the small manors and lands which have survived in name, though divorced from their ancient owners, that " Mediæval Croydon " is rich in the past.

The chief manor, descending from the times of Lanfranc, and associated with the See of Canterbury, gathers around it a lengthened history. On two occasions only has it been disconnected with the Archbishopric—once when exchanged by Cranmer for other tenures, and again by its alienation during the Commonwealth period.

Associated with this manor was the park, or " chase," presumably a hunting-ground, to which sport even Primates were addicted, and history never forgets to recall the story of Archbishop

* F. Harrison, "Annals of Sutton Place, Surrey," 1893.

Abbot and of the keeper whom he accidentally shot in Bramshill Park, while on a like expedition.

Custodians of these parks were regularly appointed, and in 1352 we read of the famous Lord Mayor of London, Sir William Walworth, as keeper at Croydon, and at times their emolument was not unsatisfactory, having a lodge, all the small wood, the bark of all trees felled, with grass for two cows, and the grand fee of twopence per day. The name of Park Hill, close to the town, keeps in memory the traditions of this " chase."

Other and smaller manorial estates claim our notice, either from their connection with Surrey worthies, or their intimate relation with local annals.

Such is Norbury, or Northborough, so called from its position north of the town. The manor remained with the Carews of Beddington till the attainder of Sir Nicholas Carew, in 1539, reverting to Francis Carew, whose entertainment of Queen Elizabeth at his Surrey mansion was marked by courtier-like elegance and display. So far did this reach, that " he kept back the ripening of cherries, by raising a tent of canvas over the tree, withholding the sun till the berries grew large, and when he was assured of her Majesty's coming he removed the tent, and a few sunny days brought them to their full maturity.[*]

Another manor, that of Haling, was let on lease in 1594 to Lord Howard of Effingham, Lord High Admiral, whose name recalls one of the heroes of the Spanish Armada; this admiral died there in 1624.

The connection of the Howard family with Effingham in Surrey has been ably treated in a paper of the Surrey Archæological Society, by Mr. G. Leveson-Gower, F.S.A.

It is well known that place-names have often had a remote origin. The somewhat ordinary one of Whitehorse, or Whitehouse (still surviving in Whitehorse Road) recalls the fact that the manor was so named from Walter Whitehorse, shield bearer to Edward III. [†]

Waddon, adjoining Croydon, is another manor, its Saxon name, supposed by Dr. Ducarel to be derived from Woden, the deity formerly worshipped there.

Other and smaller holdings there are, of

---

[*] Sir Hugh Platt's *Garden of Eden.*

[†] The manor is also called Bencham, and its gabled mansion house was north of the town towards Norwood.

which space will not allow a description, but each and all have had their share in making the past famous and significant.

Local names round Croydon point to earlier than mediæval times, and justify its remote origin even from the Roman period. Of these it may be mentioned that some antiquaries have fixed the neighbouring Woodcote, as the Noviomagus mentioned in the itinerary of Antoninus, and Scarbrook, a name of Saxon days, to "scar," meaning a steep or craggy hill, and "broc," a running water, is indicated by the fine spring that issued from the bottom of one of the hilly sides of the town.

Some roads named from local surroundings, as Windmill and Cherry Orchard roads, sufficiently illustrate their meaning, and we hasten on to the inns, which always revealed a distinct phase of a town's history. The "Crown" and "King's Arms" both tell of Royal proclivities, while the "Chequers" and the "Swan," two other hostelries, have been identified with many changeful incidents. Crosses were often placed in old towns, and here there were anciently four, to mark the boundaries of certain properties, one of these formerly stood near Handcross Alley, of which the existing Handcroft Road probably preserves some connection.

Markets and fairs were characteristics of the past, and we read of a butter market, rebuilt by Archbishop Tenison in 1708. Croydon Fair, not so long abolished, attracted in 1622 no less a personage than Edward Alleyn, playwright, and the founder of Dulwich College, for he writes at that date, " I went to Croyden fayre, dined with yᵉ Archbishop, wher ware yᵉ Dean off Pauls, and Sir Ed. Sackvile." *

Like Chester and other ancient towns, there were the " Rows " at Croydon, and " Middle Row " exists to tell its tale of bygone days, when wares of all sorts were displayed in bazaar-like fashion, a custom no doubt of eastern origin.

The High Street in olden times was much lower in level than the present thoroughfare, and extended westwards towards Beddington. Steinman remarks in his history it " was only a bridle path running through the fields." The houses had wooden steps to them, and on the rising of the little stream at Wandle, people had to cross on planks. The inhabitants in general

* Diary of Edward Alleyn, edited by W. Young, *History of Dulwich College* (May 1889).

were smiths and colliers, and the most character-
istic calling was that of the charcoal trade, which,
according to Ducarel (the local antiquary),
survived down to 1783, for he writes, " Croydon is
surrounded by hills, well covered with wood,
whereof great store of charcoal is made."

That this was a much earlier occupation is
shown by the sixteenth century writers,
prominent among whom was Alexander Barclay,
who died at Croydon in 1522, and who has
recorded :—

> " When I in youth in Croidon town did dwell,
> In Croidon I heard the collier preach." *

Other mediæval authors and playwrights have
spoken of the grimy occupations of this place, for
Greene, in his " Upstart Courtier," has, " Marry,"
quoth he, " that looke like Lucifer, though I am
black, I am not the divell, but a collyer of Croydon."

The existing Collier's Water Lane indicates a
spot where the colliers and charcoal burners
obtained a supply of water, the lane leading
directly from the dense forests which once
surrounded this place.

Richard Crowley, satirist and poet, has an
epigram on the colliers of Croydon.   The woods,

* Steinman, G. S., " History of Croydon," 1534.

almost encircling at one time the old town, must have had a long history, surviving in many names to the present day, as Woodside, Selhurst, Norwood, etc., and their recesses must have afforded, as we know they did, fine opportunity for the smuggler's trade.

Though somewhat later than the period we describe, Croydon, during the Civil War, affords a vivid picture of that loyalty for which Surrey was famous, and the town appears to have been a centre for the passing to and fro of the parliamentary armies. Sterborough Castle, on the Sussex border, surrounded by a moat, was a great stronghold, and with Farnham on the Hampshire side, supplied reinforcements which at one time or another came through this town, in 1647 the head-quarters of General Fairfax.*

The devastating power of these wars on our historical buildings was dire indeed, a fact noticed by the State papers of the day, which mention " since the introduction of railways, no events had wrought so great a change in rural England, as on the feudal seats of the nobility and gentry, during the Civil Wars." Though we have lost

---

* The recent work of Edna Lyall, " To right the wrong," a tale of the Civil War, describes many of the Surrey fortified spots and ancient roads.

several of such memorials, some remain, shewing that :—

> "Time had hallowed into beauty many a tower,
>   Which, when it frowned with all its battlements,
>   Was very terrible."

That pious foundations were not wanting to mark one of those special characteristics of mediæval history, is seen in Archbishop Whitgift's Hospital, founded in 1597, and having for its motto over the entrance gateway, "Qui dat pauperi non indigebit." The mellowed brick of this ancient building, with its gabled front and inner quadrangle, bespeaks almost to-day the Croydon of 300 years ago, and is a choice bit of antiquity left, and long may it remain.

Its dedication to the Trinity is endorsed by the lines underneath the portrait of its founder, now in the hall of the Whitgift School.

> "A striking portrait of this Primate see,
>   Who built the chapel to the Holy Three."

John Whitgift, Archbishop from 1583-1604, lived during some of the most momentous times of England's history,—descended from an ancient Yorkshire family, he was educated at Peterhouse, Cambridge, of which he became a Fellow, afterwards Lady Margaret Professor of Divinity, and

in 1567 master of Pembroke Hall, and in 1570 of
Trinity College. His preferments were rapid, from
Chaplain to the Queen he was made Dean of
Lincoln, then Bishop of that See, and on the
death of Archbishop Grindal, Primate of all
England. He lived to witness the death of his
queen in 1603, to place the crown on James I. in
Westminster Abbey, and to see the opening of
the Hampton Court conference in 1604. That
king, however, whom he had so recently crowned,
was soon present with the aged Primate, who
in his last moments exclaimed, " Pro ecclesia
Dei, pro ecclesia Dei."

His excellence in preaching was so great, and
the queen was so pleased with his discourse and
manner, as facetiously to call him her " White
gift." His close friendship with the statesmen
of the day, Burleigh, Sir Christopher Hatton,
and others, brought him into contact with many
state affairs, while it is well known that he received
from learned foreigners, especially Beza,
expressions of gratitude and respect for the
sympathy he had shown to several of their exiled
brethren for religion's sake. His entertainments
at Lambeth, Canterbury, and Croydon, were
sumptuous and on a grand scale, keeping open

house at Christmas, and entertaining his sovereign
in many of her progresses with great splendour.
It was, however, at Croydon, to which place the
Archbishop was specially attached, that he
erected the building with which his name is
inseparably connected.

Begun in 1596, in little more than three years

NORTH END AND WHITGIFT HOSPITAL, CROYDON.

the hospital was finished, the materials having
been brought from the adjoining neighbourhood,
most of the timber from Lingfield and Norwood,
the bricks from Epsom and Streatham, and the
sand from Duppas Hill. The building accounts
give an interesting idea of the expenditure and
work of those days. The statutes, framed by

the Archbishop, were ordered to be openly read
in the chapel of the hospital, and a periodical
visitation formerly took place.

The quadrangle, almost like a college enclosure,
is surrounded by the hall, the chapel, and the
warden's room, together with several apartments
for the pensioners. Old glass and panelled wood-
work vie with each other in charming colour and
excellence, and heraldic devices peep out from
many a corner window, or carved mantel, among
which the arms of the See of Canterbury occupy
an important place. The chapel has its distinctive
features, in the quaint fittings and the fine oak
wainscot, and no less has the common or dining-
room many an interesting relic.

One of Dr. Whitgift's traits of character is
related in Isaac Walton's life of Hooker.
" Whenever the queen descended to that lowliness
to dine with him at Lambeth, he would usually
the next day shew the like lowliness to his poor
brothers and sisters at Croydon, and dine with
them at his hospital at Croydon." The same
Archbishop here received in his own apartments
the Earl of Shrewsbury, Lord Zouch, the Bishop
of London, and others of exalted rank.

It is somewhat singular that the Primate's

successor, Dr. Abbot, should have founded a similar hospital at Guildford, so that two of the important Surrey towns possess buildings which are of an extremely interesting character; other examples are, Ford's Hospital near Coventry, St. Cross near Winchester, and St. John's Hospital, Northampton.

Besides the external quaintness of Whitgift's Hospital, there are many documentary relics which illustrate the annals of the institution, such as the Common Seal, bearing the story of Dives and Lazarus, the statutes which were ordered to be read in the chapel of the building, besides a great number of Court Rolls, deeds, and indentures as to property and persons. All these, by the care of the governors, have recently been put in excellent order. The alms box placed within the gateway entrance, has clasps and hinges of ancient fashion, and mention must be made of the old oaken chests, the carved mantel in the warden's room, the curious mazer bowls, and the different pieces of stained glass (some with the arms of Queen Elizabeth) which throw an old-world charm over this picture of " Bygone Surrey."

The modern Grammar School, the free school

of Whitgift's foundation, contains an excellent portrait of that Archbishop, and though the benefits of this institution are greatly enlarged since the days when the teaching was carried on in the old school house, the founder's intentions are carried out with fitting care and liberality.

Ellis Davy, citizen and mercer of London, and

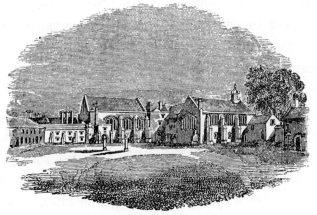

CROYDON PALACE.

founder, in 1449, of the Alms House which bears his name, is another link with Croydon of the past.

This religious and charitable establishment, whose original statutes are preserved in Archbishop Morton's register at Lambeth, survives (though rebuilt) to this day, and affords another instance of the rise of such institutions, as a distinct phase of mediæval life.

11

The Masters and Wardens of the Mercers' Company were overseers of the almshouse, whose benefactor—Elye Davy—is also commemorated by a memorial plate in the adjoining parish church.

For the advanced light that has been thrown on our old towns, their institutions and annals, through the publication of parish registers, copying inscriptions, replacing of monuments to their original site, and a better disposition to respect ancient remains, we cannot be too thankful ; at the same time, this movement ought to influence all those who are *responsible* for the preservation of our local memorials to be more jealous of the rights they are *bound* as citizens to exercise.

The late Dean Stanley * once said, " The time is come when a spirit prevails of juster appreciation of the past. It has grown up at the very moment when, but for it, every relic of antiquity would have disappeared ; . . . we may be able to hand down to future generations the gifts and inheritances we have received from generations of old."

* Address, Kent Archæological Society, 1858.

Wanborough.

By Lady West.

IF a horseman cantering on the deliciously springy turf which stretches for ten miles by the side of the old Roman road leading from Guildford (Tennyson's Astolat) to Farnham, along the top of the "Hog's Back," should draw rein to breathe his horse about half-way between those towns, and turning from the well-known view of Hind Head and the Devil's Jumps on his left, look at the wide-stretching prospect on his right, he would see beneath him, nestling among trees, almost at the foot of the hill, a collection of picturesque roofs—the little village, church, and manor house of Wanborough. Although Green, in his "*Making of England*," quoting probably from Kemble's "*Saxons in England*," says of it, that "it has in all probability been a sacred site for every form of religion which has been received into Britain, and derives its name of Wodensborough from its dedication to the grim old Saxon deity Woden," as "the famous springs of water at Wanborough are peculiarly pure, and never freeze" (Kemble), some antiquaries think the name may be derived from the word water, or Woden.

The manor was given by William the Conqueror to Sir Geoffrey de Mandeville, or Magnaville, and is mentioned in Doomsday as the property of his namesake and grandson, the turbulent and ambitious Earl of Essex, of

WANBOROUGH, FROM THE HOG'S BACK.
(Pen and ink sketch by Lady West.)

Stephen's time, who, tempted by extravagant grants, deserted the king, and joined the party of the Empress Maud.

At the head of a considerable army he laid waste the royal domains, sacked the town of Cambridge, and committed the most sacrilegious excesses at Ramsey Abbey, for which impiety he was excommunicated.

Receiving his death wound at the siege of the Royal Castle of Burnwell, he repented of his evil deeds, but sought in vain for ecclesiastical aid and benediction. At this juncture some Knights Templars took him under their protection, and after his death conveyed his body to the old Temple in London, but fearing to give him Christian burial, put the body in lead, and hung it in an apple tree.

Some years later, his absolution having been procured, they buried him in the porch of the new Temple Church, before the west door.

The effigy is believed to be the only example of a monument with the tall cylindrical flat-topped helmet over the hood of mail.

Gough describes the shield as the earliest example known of sculptured armorial bearings on a monumental effigy.

In Henry the Third's reign, the manor was sold to Gilbert, second Abbot of Waverley. Six monks were detached from the Abbey, who lived at the " cell " of Wanborough, served the parish church, and managed the farm of which the huge tithe barns, with magnificent massive timbers, are still in use.

The church, dedicated to St. Bartholomew,

was built in the time of William the Conqueror, partly of stone and flint, partly of old Roman tiles. A screen of Spanish chestnut divides the chancel from the body of the church. There are records of oblations received there from Pilgrims.

WANBOROUGH CHURCH, SURREY.
(Pen and ink sketch by Lady West.)

After the dissolution of monasteries, the church came into lay hands, but there seems to have been no endowment, and no appointment, and divine service was only occasionally performed, and for many years it was practically used as a storehouse, till it was repaired, in 1862, by Mr. Duckworth, at that time the rector of the adjoining parish of Putenham, and restored to its proper use as the Parish Church.

A great number of flint implements, now in the Charter House Museum, have been found, many of them in the "Fair Field," where a fair used to be held to supply the wants of the Canterbury Pilgrims; also Roman tiles and pottery; and on the north side of the present house, remains of walls or foundations abound at the depth of about three feet.

At the suppression of the monasteries, Henry VIII. bestowed the manor on the Earl of Southampton, who is supposed to have built the present house in 1527. It is of moderate size, is built of narrow bricks, with seven gables to the central main body, and has wings, consisting of one room each, projecting from each side, so as to enclose three sides of a courtyard. Under one of these wings a flight of steps takes you into a massively vaulted chamber, from which an underground passage (now closed), leads under the house to the church.

On the first floor a secret room has recently been discovered. It was about nine feet long, by four feet five, and the only ingress was by a door in the vast kitchen chimney, which was reached by a ladder, and concealed by the smoke. There used to be a tale in the village, that such a hiding-place existed, and it was talked of as the Covenanters' room, but no other tradition remained to account for the name. The Abbot's Pond, fed by the famous springs alluded to above, was formerly fourteen acres in extent, but has now been much reduced in size, the land reclaimed and cultivated, and the mill disused.

At Lord Southampton's death, the manor devolved on his half-brother, Sir Anthony Browne, and then changed hands rapidly by descent or purchase. At one time the Duchess of Hamilton settled it on her second husband, Thomas Dalmahoy, and the initials, T. D., separated by a heart, which are carved on the centre gable, are supposed to relate to this.

At another time it is recorded that James I., journeying with his queen from Loseley to Farnham, halted for refreshment at Wanborough, and knighted his host at the gate.

A row of "immemorial" yews, which would

seem to date from the days of the monks' hedges, adds an interesting and unusual feature to the garden, and from the terrace they overshadow a lovely view over green fields, and purple heather stretches away towards Ascot and Windsor.

Battersea and Clapham.

By Percy M. Thornton, m.p.

THE parish of Battersea extends on the south
bank of the Thames from Penge on the
west to Lambeth on the east, forming the
northern and part of the western boundary of the
sister parish of Clapham. The village of Clapham
which, in 1638, numbered forty-six ratepayers
only, was situated on high ground on the south
side of the Wandsworth Road, up to which, in
ancient times, the Thames nearly reached at
highest tide.

A large part of Battersea parish was formerly
more or less under water before the low ground
was drained and reclaimed from the river, which
may have been effected during the Roman
occupation. Perhaps the canal which Canute cut
in 1016 from Limehouse Reach to St. George's
Reach, through Nine Elms (the eastern end of
Battersea parish), in order to get his ships above
London Bridge, assisted the process.

From the time of the Conquest to the dissolution

of religious houses, the manors of Battersea and Wandsworth belonged to the Abbey of Westminster. The name, originally *Patricesy* (as spelt in the Conqueror's survey), then Batrichsey, meant "(Saint) Peter's Island," Westminster Abbey being dedicated to St. Peter. King Charles I. granted the manors to Viscount Grandison, who died in 1630 ; and from him they devolved on his great-nephew, who granted them to his uncle, Walter St. John, the grandfather of Henry, Viscount Bolingbroke, Queen Anne's minister, in the possession of whose family they remained until 1763, when they were purchased for an ancestor of Earl Spencer, the present lord of the manor. Bolingbroke House, the family residence of the St. John's, stood near what is now Mr. Dives' flour-mill. Part of it, including the "Cedar Chamber," a room wainscotted with cedar, is still standing, and will always be celebrated as the place where Bolingbroke, the elder Pitt (afterward Lord Chatham), and Pope used to meet.

In the year 1868 it became necessary for sanitary reasons to disturb the crypt, and accordingly a faculty was obtained for the re-arrangement of the remains under St. Mary's

church. The dust of the famous minister was straightway placed under the crypt below the communion table. To mark the spot this inscription was placed on a raised stone tablet:—
"Henry St. John, Viscount Bolingbroke, Secretary of State to Queen Anne. Born 1678, died 1751."

In the fifteenth century, Thomas, Lord Stanley, had property in Battersea, but in 1461 some of it was made over to Lawrence Booth, Bishop of Durham, who, in 1477, became Archbishop of York. In 1472, the king gave the Bishop some property, which Lord Stanley had forfeited under the statute of mortmain. The residence of the Archbishop of York on this property was formerly called Bridge House, and subsequently York House.

Dr. Church, a distinguished divine, who took an active part in the Wesley and Middleton controversy, was vicar of Battersea 1740-1756.

In Battersea Fields (now Battersea Park), the Duke of Wellington fought his duel with Lord Winchelsea in 1829.

Famous enamels used to be produced at Battersea; and the horizontal windmill, with ninety-six sets of arms, was a noteworthy object in Lyson's time, viz., 1792. A hundred years ago the parish contained market gardens covering three hundred acres.

The Old Bridge, built over the ferry in 1766, was a picturesque feature of " Bygone Battersea," and is now superseded by the handsome structures opened by the late Lady Rosebery in 1890.

Now as to Clapham. The old parish church of St. Mary (on the site of which St. Paul's now stands), the old manor house, and the Cock Inn, which still retains some of the sixteenth century structure, were grouped together nearly due north of the new parish church of Holy Trinity, erected in 1775 at the north-east angle of the Common.

The old church has long ago vanished, giving way to the modern fane of St. Paul's, but the very interesting monument of Sir Richard Atkins and his family was discovered in 1885 in a vault or crypt, and was placed in St. Paul's by the exertions of the author of *Old Clapham*, the late Mr. J. W. Grover. Sir Richard Atkins was grandson of Henry Atkins, physician to James I. Dr. Atkins bought the manor for £6000, and his lineal descendants held it for more than a century, when it passed to Richard Bowyer, great grandfather of Rev. T. W. Atkins-Bowyer, late rector of the parish, and sometime Lord of the

Manor.   The sculptured and recumbent figures of
the Atkins' monument are of Sir Richard, dressed
as an officer of the time of Charles II., and of his
wife, Dame Rebecca, of their son Henry, aged
twenty-four, in a wig and the costume of a Roman
general, and of their daughter Annabella, aged
nineteen, and of another daughter, Rebecca, aged
nine, all in white marble, and admirable specimens
of the sculptor's art in the Stuart times.   Of the
old   manor   house,   a   handsome   Elizabethan
structure, nothing now remains except the bow
window of a girls' school, part of the base of an
octagonal tower; which gave rise to the name
" Turret Grove."

There are other remains of ancient buildings,
and several houses designed by Sir Christopher
Wren; but the chief interest of Bygone Clapham
is human, rather than archæological; and though
tradition (as to which the writer is sceptical),
asserts that Cromwell and Captain Cooke
resided in the village, while General Ireton
certainly lived there for a time; and though
Nicholas Brady, of Psalmodic fame, was rector
1706-1726; and though, according to the late
Mr. Grover, " Clapham was the seat of a Danish
nobleman, Osgod Clapa, at the marriage feast of

whose daughter King Hardicanute fell senseless
to the ground in a fit of intoxication, and expired,"
we must revert to the Common for the most
famous and familiar worthies of Clapham.

A large portion of this fine expanse of turf and
once, alas, of gorse, interspersed with noble trees,
which attracted so many to the locality since the
Restoration, and especially since Queen's Anne's
accession, belongs to Battersea Parish; the
Battersea boundary running from Wix's Lane to
the Mount Pond.

By a compensatory coincidence, the house which
was successively the home of "Single Speech"
Hamilton, of Henry Thornton, of Wilberforce, of
Sir Robert H. Inglis, the library of which Pitt
designed, the house which, more than any other
building, is associated with the abolition of slavery,
the colonisation of Sierra Leone, missions to India,
the Church Missionary Society, and the centre of
the evangelical movement, is known as *Battersea
Rise*, though it belongs to Clapham borough, and
is on that common.

But before we come to the illustrious " Clapham
Sect," chronological sequence invites us to name
Gauden House, a large mansion standing in
extensive grounds, built shortly after the

Restoration, to the west of The Chase, by Sir
Dennis Gauden, brother of Bishop Gauden,
who was thought to be the real author of the
Eikon Basilike. On Sir Dennis' death in 1688,
the estate was purchased by a retired commissioner
of the navy, William Hewer, who had been clerk
to Samuel Pepys. After the Revolution, Pepys
lived in Mr. Hewer's house in retirement, and
died there in 1703. He speaks of the house as
"almost built" in his diary.

The house was pulled down soon afterwards,
and the estate is now occupied by the Terrace and
Victoria Road. Its famous neighbour, " The
Cedars," designed by Christoper Wren or Inigo
Jones, survived until 1864, and gave the name to
Cedars Road.

The house where Granville Sharp, the
abolitionist, is said to have resided, was completed
in 1720, and most of the houses in Church
Buildings are still in good condition. The
portion now known as No. 3 and No. 4, was
Lord Macaulay's first school. He was a day
scholar under Mr. Greaves, who started his
scholastic work, under the auspices of the
philanthropist, by trying to educate youths from
Africa. To a school in Church Building, Tom

Hood also resorted, and avenged himself for this captivity within the "irksome walls" in his "Ode on a Distant Prospect of Clapham Academy"— thus described :—

> "Ah me! those old familiar bounds!
>   That classic house, those classic grounds,
>   My pensive thought recalls.
>   What tender urchins now confine,
>   What little captives now repine
>   Within yon irksome walls."

John Thornton, the merchant-prince and philanthropist, was born on the border of Clapham Common, in 1720. He was a son and successor of Robert Thornton, a merchant in the Russian trade, at Hull, who had a villa on Clapham Common.

John Thornton is chiefly celebrated for his great munificence, and the unsectarian character of his piety; yet he may be regarded as the father of the so-called "Clapham Sect;" for he was the father of Henry Thornton, who purchased Battersea Rise in the year 1792, while Wilberforce, also of Hull, having lived at Wimbledon with his aunt, Mrs. Wilberforce, for some years of his boyhood, and having been subsequently a frequent guest at John Thornton's

12

house at Clapham, formed an early friendship for
Henry Thornton, which exercised a potent
influence on the life and characters of both.
John Thornton's three sons were all highly
respected Members of Parliament, and his only
daughter married Lord Balgony, and became
Countess of Leven and Melville. Samuel
Thornton, John's eldest son, was Pitt's financial
adviser, successively member for Hull and Surrey,
as well as long a governor of the Bank of England,
he lived through five reigns, viz., George II.
to Victoria—1754-1838. Robert, the second
son, was M.P. for Colchester, and inhabited
a large house, the site of which is now
occupied by the Nunnery. The third son,
Henry, of Battersea Rise, the friend and
coadjutor of Wilberforce, entered parliament in
1784, when still a young man, four years after
Wilberforce, as member for the borough of
Southwark, and as an independent politician,
giving a general support to Pitt. He was, for
thirty years, second only to Horner as an
authority on Currency and Finance. His public
and private character are well illustrated by his
writings, for he was the author of a standard
work on paper credit, of a Book of Family

Prayers, which is still largely used, and of commentaries on the Old and New Testaments. He also contributed a number of political and moral essays to the *Christian Observer*, and composed tracts for Hannah More. He drew his friend Wilberforce to Clapham, where they lived together for several years, and gathered around them a remarkable circle of public benefactors. The genius and impetuosity of Wilberforce, allied to the science and common sense of Thornton, were irresistible. Charles Grant, an influential director of the East India Company, and Eliot, Pitt's brother-in-law, became their neighbours in the two houses built by Henry Thornton on either side of his own residence. After Eliot's death and Henry Thornton's marriage, in 1787, Wilberforce succeeded Eliot as tenant of Broom field, now Broomwood.

It was at this time that Mr. Pitt designed the oval library in Mr. Thornton's house on Battersea Rise, which stands, as Sir James Stephen says in his famous essay, "a solitary monument of the architectural skill of that imperial mind."

The society at Clapham included among its prominent members Zachary Macaulay, the secretary of the anti-slavery movement, and the

editor of the *Christian Observer*, who lived at
No. 5, The Pavement, at the north-east angle of
the Common, where Sir George Trevelyan tells
us the future Lord Macaulay passed "a happy
childhood," and Granvill Sharp, of Church
Buildings, and Lord Teignmouth, at what is now
the convent, and James Stephen, father of a
Clapham worthy, Sir James Stephen, of Stowey
House, who drafted the Abolition Bill of 1833;
on the south side of the common the elder Charles
Grant, Thomas Babington, Charles Simeon,
and John Venn, Rector of Clapham, and later on
John Bowdler. Of this set, Macaulay in 1844
wrote as follows :—

" From that little knot of men emanated all the
bible societies and almost all the missionary
societies in the world. The whole organization of
the Evangelical party was their work. The share
that they had in providing means for the education
of the people was great. They were really the
destroyers of the slave trade and slavery. Many
of those whom Stephen describes were public men
of the greatest weight. Lord Teignmouth governed India at Calcutta; Grant governed India at
Leadenhall Street; Stephen's father was Percival's
right-hand man in the House of Commons. It is

needless to speak of Wilberforce. As to Simeon, if you knew what his authority and influence were, and how they extended from Cambridge to the most remote corners of England, you would allow that his sway in the church was greater than that of any primate."

While these earnest Claphamites were studying men and manners, and labouring to save souls, the great chemist and natural philosopher, Henry Cavendish, grandson of the second Duke of Devonshire, at Cavendish House, close to the south angle of the common, was analysing air and water, and there found the means, if not for lifting, at any rate for weighing the earth. He was amassing the while out of an already ample fortune, more than a million sterling by mere disregard of wealth and luxury.

Zachary Macaulay, son of the Presbyterian minister of Cardross, became governor of Sierra Leone in 1792, and on his return in 1799, settled at Clapham, as secretary to the Directors of the Colony, and in 1800 editor of the *Christian Observer*. Of his son, Lord Macaulay, it need only be said here that he was of Clapham, by early education and residence. Sir John Shore, a Harrovian, and contemporary of Sir William

Jones, when Lord Teignmouth succeeded Lord Cornwallis as governor general of India, and on his return to England in 1797 was made an Irish peer. With Mr. Henry Thornton he took part in raising a large corps of volunteers on the threatened invasion by Napoleon I.

After Henry Thornton's death, in 1815, Mr. (afterwards Sir) Robert Harry Inglis, Bart., member for Oxford University, 1829-1859, with his wife settled at Battersea Rise until 1833, taking charge of the nine orphans, and made it "the resort of many people of note and genius who either dwelt in London or visited it."

Clapham has reason to be proud of its Nonconformist divines. In the seventeenth century Dr. Wilkinson and Mr. Lye attracted congregations here. The adherents of the latter subsequently assembled in Clapham Hall, which was erected as a chapel in 1769. From 1710 to 1807 three distinguished ministers, Rev. M. Lowman, Dr. Philip Furneaux, and Rev. Thomas Urwick, successively preached at Clapham Hall, whence in 1852 the congregation moved to Grafton Square Chapel.

A notable high-churchman finds a place on the Clapham roll of fame, having been born in

Broomwood House, namely Samuel Wilberforce, son of the philanthropist, successively Bishop of Oxford and Winchester.

The Rev. John Venn, born in Clapham in 1759, was a most eloquent preacher, and one of the distinguished divines of the Evangelical party. His successor, Dr. William Dealtry, was Archdeacon of Surrey and Chancellor of the Diocese of Winchester. In scholarship and theology, he was equally eminent, and all his various gifts of learning and eloquence were freely expended in promoting the best interests of the parish. It is truly said in his epitaph " His labours in this parish, recorded in the churches and schools erected during his incumbency, and in benevolent associations established through his efforts, have left their testimony in the hearts of those for whom he was ever ready to spend and to be spent in the service of the Lord."

Sir Charles Trevelyan, a distinguished Indian administrator, lived on the common near Battersea Rise ; Sir James Stephen, already mentioned, wrote the celebrated essay on the Clapham Sect for the *Edinburgh Review*, reprinted in his *Essays on Ecclesiastical Biography* (Longman's 1867). The Elms House, which when this was first written was situated at the corner of The Chase, was in former times the residence of the Barclays, so distinguished for wealth, probity, and religious fervour, who, like the Hanburys of Clapham, traced their descent from King Edward I. At the Elms, in 1860, after ten years residence, died Sir Charles Barry, the distinguished architect of the Houses of Parliament. Field-Marshal Sir George Pollock resided at Beechwood, on the west side of the common in Battersea Parish, and died there in 1872. It is appropriate that the man who enjoys the chief credit for mitigating the rigour of our criminal code, namely, Sir James Macintosh, should have taken up his abode at Battersea Rise; to wit, in the house called "Maisonette," where Wilberforce visited him in 1830.

The late Mr. Henry Sykes Thornton, Henry Thornton's son, amply maintained the family traditions of intellectual ability, business capacity, religious earnestness, and munificent philanthropy.

Clapham has grown very rapidly during the last hundred years. When Wilberforce and Henry Thornton entered Parliament there were, it is said, only 240 houses in the parish, while in 1885 there were 6263 houses; and now there are probably over 7000, while the old houses of past worthies are fast disappearing, and their grounds being laid out for building purposes.

The following interesting items are from H. A. Batten's "Key and Companion to the Plan of Clapham," 1827 :—

1698.—March 12th being Fast day, the following brief was read : The Vaudois inhabitants of the valley on the side of the river Clusa, who being subjects of France before the late war, have, since the conclusion of the peace, through Papish cruelty, been exiled and banished from their native country, without any present hopes to return, but by renouncing their holy religion, which through the singular goodness of Almighty God, both they and their brethren, the Vaudois of Pedmont, on the other side of the same river, have hitherto kept undefiled.

The Collection made was - £126 0 0

1704.—For the Distressed Protestants in the Principality of Orange, on which occasion £13 18 6. was collected at the doors of the Church, and £41 19 6½ at the Dissenting meeting.

1793.—May 12th. For the French emigrants
from house to house - £131 0 0

1807 —Nov. 22nd. For the British Prisoners
in France - - - £87 19 9

1826.—April 30th. For the distressed Silk Weavers
in Spitalfields - - £105 13 0

1826.—April 30th. At St. Paul's Chapel - £95 0 0

Nonsuch.

By S. W. Kershaw, f.s.a.

"That which no equal has in art or fame,
Britons deservedly do Nonsuch name."

THE story goes that Henry VIII., hunting
near the Banstead downs, when tired of
the chase, was entertained by Sir Richard de
Cuddington, who owned that Manor. The King
was so pleased with the place, he offered an
exchange, annexed the manor to Hampton Court,
and built a palace on the site, a palace whose
fame has long been a bye-word for quaint and
original beauty.

The erection of Nonsuch marks an epoch in
artistic history, the fairy-like structure which
was the pride of the Tudors, claims the genius of
Italy in its varied designs, and its wealth of
ornament is a striking illustration of the influence
of foreign taste on English architecture.

In the earliest description of Nonsuch, in 1582,
"it is stated Henry VIII. procured many
artificers, architects, sculptors, and statuaries, as
well as Italians, French, and Dutch, who

applied to the ornament of this mansion the finest and most curious skill they possessed in their several arts, embellishing it within and without with magnificent statues, some of which represent the antiquities of Rome," and some surpass them, a statement which Camden in his "Britannia" echoes, and declares that Nonsuch "was built with so much splendour and elegance, that it stands a monument of art, and you would think that the skill and science of architecture were exhausted on this one building. It has such a profusion of animated statues and finished pieces of art, rivalling the ornaments of ancient Rome itself, that it justly receives and maintains its name from them."

The credit of the design rests with one Anthonio or Toto* dell Nunciata, a Florentine painter and architect, who entered, with many other foreign artists, the King's service, and whose special skill in designing allegorical and pictorial sculpture was seen in the elaborate ornament, which justly earned for this building the name of "Nonsuch," a palace of which, it may be said, it was the only one Henry VIII.

---

* The "Denizations," Huguenot Society of London, 1893, mention a grant to Anthony Toto and his wife, of cottages and land at Mitcham.

built. To the engraved view, taken from Hoefnagel's print of 1582, may be added the following minute description :—

"The original and principal structure was of two stories, the lower being of substantial and well wrought freestone, and the upper of wood, richly adorned and set forth and garnished with a variety of statues, pictures (*i.e.*, coloured figures in relief), and other artistic forms of excellent art and workmanship, and of no small cost. Its roof is covered with blue slate. In the centre, over the gatehouse to the inner court, was a clock turret, and at either end of the structure, east and west, was a large tower of five stories high, commanding an extensive prospect. . . . This singular building remained in good condition for more than a century, for it is noticed both by Evelyn and Pepys in their diaries in the year 1665. The palace consists of two courts, of which the first is of stone, castle like, built in the reign of Elizabeth, by Lord Lumley ; the other of timber, a Gothic fabric, but the walls incomparably beautiful. The appearing timber, entrelaces, etc., were all so covered with scales of slate, that it seemed carved in the wood and painted, the slate fastened on the timbers in pretty figures, that has, like a coat of armour, preserved it from rotting. There stand in the garden two handsome stone pyramids."*

Documentary evidence proves the vast amount of work expended on the palace, and we note in 1542 a "Bill of charges by carvers and gilders done at Nonsuch,"† as one of the many items expended on this royal domain.

From the same source one gleans much concerning the building materials : the stone was brought from Reigate, also Caen and Luke stone, were conveyed by water, and landed at Ditton on the Thames. The timber was principally supplied from the Wealden district, or from woods near, as we read of its carriage from Horley, Bristow, Lee (Leigh), Bowkham (Bookham). The principal pieces for the towers at Nonsuch were from Rusper on the Sussex border, and there are charges for felling and sawing of timber at the above place, and at New-digate. These paymasters' accounts also mention smiths' work, sawyers and chalk diggers, besides an infinity of smaller expenses, all very interesting, attesting the fact that on the erection of such a

---

* *Gentleman's Magazine*, August 1837.
† Domestic State Papers, Henry VIII.

house, *local* resources were employed, and that as one of the King's manors, the enrolment of its expenses in the State papers, gives it a first rank in Surrey antiquarian lore.

Every portion seems to have received minute attention in decorative details, and to have exemplified this feature more forcibly than Hampton Court or Whitehall, also filled with so called "pictures," but as mentioned above, they were more properly bas-reliefs in wood or alabaster plaques, tapestry, needlework, and all those decorations which received a direct impetus from the influence of foreign workmen.

The excessive patronage of "strangers," naturally caused dissatisfaction, a sentiment expressed in the rhyming ballads of the day :—

> "Poor tradesmen had small dealings then,
> And who but strangers bore the bell,
> Which was a grief to Englishmen,
> To see them here in London dwell."

To construct the clock which adorned the central tower of Nonsuch, six French artisans were sent for, and their names are to be found in the "Letters and Denizations," 1509-1603, before mentioned.

At this time there were few clockmakers in

England, most of them came from Normandy, and the old turret clock at Hampton Court bears the initials of Nicholas Oursiau, a foreigner.

Gardens and lawns surrounded Nonsuch, and many a fantastically wrought fountain sparkled in the fair quadrangle, or on the broad terraced walk of this stately manor.

Long varied banks and alleys of trellis work diversified the scene, and it is said that Lord Bacon had this unique picture in his mind when he wrote his "Essays of Buildings and of Gardens."

Hentzner, whose travels are far famed, describing his visit, says "two fountains, one round and the other like a pyramid, upon which are perched small birds that stream water out of their bills; in the grove of Diana is a fountain and nymphs with inscription; there is besides, another pyramid of marble, full of concealed pipes which spirts upon all who come within their reach!"

Camden writes:—

"The house is surrounded with parks full of deer, delicate orchards and gardens, groves adorned with arbours, little garden-beds and walks shaded with trees, that pleasure and health seem to have made choice of this place, and to live together."

The manor of Cheam has had its roll of fame. Henry the VIII. exchanged it with Cranmer for lands at Chislet in Kent. The living has also been noted, for five of its rectors, in the sixteenth and seventeenth centuries became bishops, and of them, Lancelot Andrews and Bishop Hacket of Lichfield were most eminent. Of the former, the witty Fuller remarked that "they who stole his sermons could not steal his manner." Elizabeth made him Dean of Wells, and he had great share in the revision of the Bible in 1611. His ability and learning found vent in the couplet,

> "If ever any merited to be
> The universal Bishop, this was he,"

and one of the famed monuments in St. Saviour's, Southwark, is to Bishop Andrews.

After the death of Henry VIII., the Earl of Arundel, whose descendants are commemorated in the celebrated Lumley monuments and brasses, in the adjoining church of Cheam, possessed Nonsuch.

Near at hand an ancient house called "Whitehall," was famous for having been either an appendage for the court attendants, or for occasional use by royalty itself.

Lord Lumley was a great collector, and a most

interesting association constantly occurs in the fact that many of Archbishop Cranmer's works were acquired by Lord Lumley, whose autograph with that of the martyr Primate repeatedly appears on the title pages.

The correspondence of the Earl of Arundel with Sir William More, is to be found in the famous collection known as the "Loseley MSS." extending from the twelfth to the seventeenth century, and that mine of chronicled lore and political gossip was gathered in the historic house of Loseley, than which no more typical illustration of "bygone" art and architecture exists, even to-day, in this, one of the fairest mansions in all Surrey.

It was from Lord Arundel that Elizabeth purchased Nonsuch, and became so enamoured of the place. Long before her tenure, this house had played a varied and important part in English annals, "the manor of Nonsuch" being a frequent appendage to many a state paper, news-letter, or Royal despatch. In 1555 we read Queen Mary's permission was given to M. Noailles, the French ambassador, to see the gardens and park; another time we read of a warrant to deliver to him two does from the Great Park, and to her cousin, Cardinal Pole, the Queen wrote a letter, under

13

royal signet, permitting him to hunt deer in the park.

As time progresses, we find mention of several offices connected with this mansion; Sir Thomas Cawarden, "Master of the Revels," was keeper of the palace and park in the reigns of Henry VIII., Edward, and Elizabeth, his friend and executor was Sir Wm. More, of Loseley, and it is of much interest to note that under Sir Thomas, a school of actors had been formed, who, it appears, were indirectly connected with the rise of the Blackfriars Theatre, and so with that of the great Shakespeare himself.

Henry VIII.'s license permitted Sir Thomas to have a company of armed retainers; his feudal estate at Blechingley further associates him with "Bygone Surrey," as well as his friendship with Sir William More, whose "zeal and pleasure," shown in all local matters, claims for the owners of Loseley, a very distinguished place in historic and county annals.

During the Earl of Arundel's tenure of Nonsuch, he entertained the Queen splendidly in 1579. Strype writes :—" Here the Queen had great entertainment, with banquets, together with a masque, and the warlike sound of drums and flutes, and all kinds of music till midnight; at night was a play of the children of St. Paul's, and their master, after that, a costly banquet, accompanied with drums and flutes, and the Earl presented Her Majesty with a cupboard of plate."

These expressions of goodwill were shown, though in another way, to Archbishop Parker, to whom the Earl gave an order to deliver deer from his estate. At this time, we read much of the Park at Nonsuch, of which there appears to have been a "Great and Little Park." In 1605 a regulation was made to endow lands for the enlargement of the park, and for some years later the State Papers record many an incident relating to its maintenance, also as to the Lodge, such as "timber for the repair," and a "warrant for sale of trees in Chute Forest, Hampshire, as well as £150 to build a fair lodge in Nonsuch Park."

Queen Elizabeth took possession of Nonsuch about 1580, and here, until her death, the Court often repaired, whence despatches were constantly dated, the letters of the famous Lord Howard of Effingham, concerning the Armada, and other like correspondence, are among the most notable.

On the second outbreak of the Spaniards, after the
great invasion, Rowland Whyte reports, " Our
fleet goes to sea ; Sir Walter Raleigh took leave
at Court of all the ladies and his friends ; he was
brought to see the singularities of the gardens,
which pleased him infinitely."

At this historical house were dated some of
the letters concerning the fate of Mary
Stuart, from Secretary Davison to the Earl of
Leicester.

In less than a month afterwards, the Earl of
Essex rode hastily along those noble avenues to
the entrance court, eager to lay the report of his
management in Ireland before the Queen.   In
that early summer morning, Essex had taken
horse from Westminster, and stirred not till he
arrived at the gates of Nonsuch, and although
the Queen was but " newly up " he obtained an
audience.   Her Majesty gave him " good words
and said he was welcome, and willed him to rest
after so wearie a journey."   " Essex thanked God
that although he had suffered much trouble and
storms abroad, he found sweet calm at home."

That fickle Queen, when the Earl waited on
her later in the afternoon, " ordered him to keep
his chamber."   Essex was in reality a prisoner

here, but he was visited and consoled by his good friend Francis Bacon, who was then in attendance at court.

Sir Nicolas Bacon, lawyer, wit, and courtier, and keeper of the Great Seal, received the Queen at his house at Gorhambury in 1577, who, when she told him it was too little for him, elicited from him the remarkable answer " No madam, it is your Highness had made me too great for my house."

The council which terminated the fate of Essex, sat at Nonsuch, and when, in after days, the Queen heard of his revolt and attempt at the overthrow of the Crown, all her fiery Tudor nature arose within her, and she exclaimed to her Chancellor Harrington, " By God's son, I am no Queen, this man is above me."

Soon after this, we read of few events at Nonsuch, and, if the story be true, riding on a sun-glaring day, the Queen thought the Palace was on fire, and on her attendants telling her it was only the sun's rays on the roof, the mistake so displeased her vanity, that she rode home and bade adieu with her Court to Nonsuch for ever. This foible, though small, stamps the extra-ordinary nature of a sovereign who, in other ways, brought England to such a height of

renown, and who had made her throne one
of the first in the world.

James I. and Anne of Denmark lived here
at various times, but "Theobalds," on the way to
Newmarket, was a more attractive resort of that
pleasure-loving king. Though Hampton Court
was the favourite abode of Charles I., occasional
allusions are made to his sojourn at Nonsuch—
certainly as recorded by Miss Strickland in her
lives of the Queens of England—"the king and
Henrietta Maria seem to have retired here, after
a somewhat paltry little quarrel on the dismissal
of the Queen's French attendants, whose retention
gave great offence to the general public."

The Palace was a retreat for court favourites ;
in 1625 we read of the Duke of Buckingham being
here to "confirm his health," and a few years
before, the Spanish Ambassador, Gondomar, on
account of his countenance of the mass, was so
unpopular, that he retired here to avoid the fury
of the people.

The Civil War brought its consequent train of
events. This mansion, with other crown lands,
fell into the hands of the commissioners, and in
1648 the following order was issued "to send out
scouts to discover whether there be any movements

of the enemy towards surprising Oatlands, Richmond, and Nonsuch, and to prevent the execution of that design." It is probable that these houses not so fortified escaped the attacks made on the greater strongholds of Farnham, Guildford, and Sterborough castles, all of which underwent a siege.

Nonsuch came under the parliamentary tenure, and a minute survey made in 1650 gives a very fair idea of its condition. Each part is described in detail, giving an excellent notion of the size and use of the numerous rooms, which accommodated so large a court retinue as had been lately maintained by Henrietta Maria. Nor are the fountains, the gardens, and the smaller buildings omitted in this survey, which is printed in Archæologia (vol v.), 1779, and of which but a fragment is here given :—

" The gatehouse leading into the outward court aforesaid, is a building very strong and gracefull, being three stories high, leaded overhead, battled and turretted in every of the four corners thereof, the highest of which stories contains a very large and spacious roome, very pleasant and delectable for prospect.

And also consisting of one other faire and very curious structure or building of two stories high, the lower story whereof is of good and well wrought free stone, and the higher of wood, richly adorned and set forth and garnished with variety

of statues, pictures,　　*　　*　　*　　all　which incloseth one
faire and large court,　　*　　*　　*　　all paved with free
stone, commonly called the Inner Court :"

.　　.　　.　　.　　.　　.　　.　　.　　.

"And also consisting of one structure of timber building of
a quadrengular forme, pleasantly situated upon the highest
parte of the said Nonsuch Parke, commonly called the
Banquetting House, being compassed round with a brick wall,
the four corners whereof represent four half moons or fortified
angles ; this building being of three stories high,　*　*　*
the stanchions and out postes of which banquetting house are
all covered with lead ; over the thirde story, there is a lanthorne
placed, covered with lead, and in every of the four corners of
the whole house a *belcone* placed for prospect."

From the above description, it would appear
that the "banquetting house" was detached from
the main building, and placed so as to serve
equally for outpost as a dining chamber ; disposed
somewhat after the Italian manner, then in vogue.
This is strengthened by the fact that the fashion
of dining together in the great hall was, in the
16th century, falling into disuse, greater prominence being given to the so-called "banquetting
house."

Ordinances for the Royal household in 1526
state that "sundrie noblemen and gentlemen doe
much delighte, and use to dyne in corners and
secret places, and not repayring to the King's
chamber or hall."

The Park is so often mentioned in the State papers of the 17th century, that it almost claims a chapter for itself.

Henry VIII. made the two parks, called the Great and Little Parks—at one time they were partly turned into tillage, and strong measures were taken to impark them again, and enlarge their area, so much that several warrants were granted for land to extend the boundaries; the two lodges were repaired, enlarged, and improvements were constant. Worcester Park was included in the Great Park, attached to Nonsuch, but was sold about 1750. The Survey then states :—

"The trees within the Parke aforesaid, already marked forth for the use of the navie, are found to be in number two thousand eight hundred and five, two hundred whereof growe so neare unto Nonsuch house, and in such a decent order, being a speciall ornament thereunto, that the cutting down thereof will not only very much impayre the magnificence of the structure, but will also exceedingly detract from the pleasantness of the seate which we humbly make bould to certifie."

We hear of Nonsuch again in 1663, when Pepys writes, that he saw a famous race on Banstead Downs, rode through Epsom, and then goes through Nonsuch Park to the House

" looks through the great gates, and found a noble court."

Three years later, the fire of London raged, and to this Surrey mansion the Exchequer's money was sent for safety.

Pepys again describes it as a " fine palace and prospect, a great walk of elm and walnut, set one after another in order, all the house has the outside filled with figures of stories, the house covered with lead and gilded." His brother diarist, Evelyn, always more minute in his artistic descriptions, " took an exact view of the plaster statues and bas-relievos, inserted 'twixt the timbers and stanchions of the outside walls of the court, which must needs have been the work of some celebrated Italian. I much admired how it lasted so well, and entire since the time of Henry VIII., exposed as they are to the air. . . There are some mezzo-relievos as big as the life ; the story is of the heathen gods, emblems, compartments, etc."

There stand in the garden two handsome stone pyramids, and the avenue is planted with rows of fair elms, but the rest of the goodly trees of this and Worcester Park adjoining were felled by those destructive rebels in the late war, and thus was defaced one of the stateliest seats his Majesty possessed. In the gardens, there was a fountain set about in six lilacs, and these have been said to be the first lilacs brought into England. Charles II. gave Nonsuch to the Duchess of Cleveland,—then its historic days are over, for to feed her extravagance, that unprincipled favourite sold the materials, with which the Earl of Berkeley erected the "Durdans" at Epsom, afterwards destroyed by fire in 1764. It was hardly to be expected otherwise of the Duchess, " who when she had a point to gain with the king, had resource either to smiles or rage, as the case might require."

The Duke of Grafton, afterwards acquired the property, and it went through various changes till the year 1803, when the present modern and elegant house, designed by Jeffrey Wyattville, was built, and the owner, Captain Farmer, J.P., now resides there.

Notes on Guildford.

By Frank Lasham.

A LTHOUGH the town of Guildford can boast of some antiquity, it must have been but a village when, about 880 A.D., it is mentioned as being a Royal Manor, and we find King Alfred bequeathing it to his nephew. Ethelwald, and it shortly after reverted to the Crown.

The evidence is very slight as to the Romans ever having been at Guildford. No coins or any other remains having been found, which would give indications of their presence. And yet, not far off, at Farley Heath, near Albury, was an extensive Romano-British camp or town. It is far from unlikely that Guildford, in Roman days, was somewhat inaccessible, being in the centre of what must have been a densely wooded district. A Roman Villa has been discovered at Chidding-fold, and evidences of a settlement have been traced on Puttenham Common, about four miles from Guildford; but with regard to the town itself, it may be said the Romans did not settle there. The Saxons seem to have been present; and it is probable that the name of the town arose from the fact that some companies or fraternities called "Guild Merchants," settled on the banks of the Wey, and took toll of merchandise and wayfarers who passed across the river; and hence the origin of the name Guildford. In 1037, when the Danes were in possession of the Crown, a massacre of King Alfred's attendants seems to have taken place at Guildford, and it is stated that some 600 Normans were here basely destroyed. In 1087 mention is made of the town, when Domesday states that :—" In Gildeforde King William hath LXXV messuages or tenements, in which are resident CLXXV Tenants."

The early residents were doubtless tenants under homage, engaged in trade, but free of the town.

The greater part of Guildford was situated then on the west side of the River Wey, and not as now. The Royal Domain or King's Chase being on the west side, it was natural that the inhabitants should reside near what must have been to them a means of subsistence.

The rest of the Royal Domain which lay on

this side of the river was reserved for the King's
private use, and was converted into a Park by
Henry II., who added some palatial buildings to
the Castle, in which he and many of the
subsequent sovereigns kept their court.   Part of
the domain on the eastern side of the town was
occupied by the Castle, part alienated to the
family of Testard, from one of whose successors it
became known as the manor of Poyle, and the
remainder disposed of to make room for the
Priory, which was founded by Queen Eleanor,
Consort of Henry II.

It appears that a charter of Henry III., granted to the town, speaks of "approved men" as
already in existence.   If so, there must have been
a body politic already then in existence, and we
may safely affirm that the town had been in
possession of Corporate rights long before the
reign of Henry III.

The Castle.

The Castle of Guildford, of which now scarcely
anything but the square Keep remains, originally
occupied a considerable eminence to the south of
the site of the present High Street, and was very
extensive :   the domestic buildings have now

nearly all disappeared. Very few authentic records as to its foundations are extant, but it is spoken of as taking the place of a Saxon fortress or stockade, and was built about the time of Henry II. The Keep is built upon an artificial mound of chalk, which was at one time surrounded by a double ditch, the inner part of which is still in existence. It is evident from the situation and general features of the Castle that it must have been built to overawe or protect the neighbourhood. Situated as it is, near the ford of the river Wey, it had an important influence over the district. Its construction would seem to indicate a close resemblance to that of Rochester, erected by Bishop Gundulph, it may therefore be considered to be about the same age. The Castle is mentioned in the reign of King John, 1216 when it seems to have been captured by Prince Louis the Dauphin of France. About 1299 it was used as a common prison for the King's prisoners. In the first year of the reign of Richard II., Sir Simon Burleigh, " sage and wise," was its Constable. Gradually the Castle appears to have lost its grandeur, and from having been a palace, appears more than ever to have degenerated and become a very common prison, for in the reign of Henry VII. it was crowded with malefactors from the counties of Surrey and Sussex. In the reign of James I. it appears to have been granted to the family of Carter, who did their best to raze it to the ground. One of the descendants of this family appears to have been dis-franchized and dismissed from the freedom of the Corporation of the Town. The Keep and grounds are now the property of the Corporation, having been purchased by them from Lord Grantley.

With regard to the structure of the Keep, the original access to the interior was on the first story, reached by a flight of stairs from the exterior. The Keep is of quadrangular shape, and its walls are in many places over ten feet thick. The ascent to the battlements was made by a circular staircase on the north-west side. Originally there were three stories, the lower used for prisoners, and the second and third floors were for the residence of the governor. Within the thickness of the walls are several chambers, and among them is an oratory, on the walls of which are some curious carvings, in the chalk, of a semi-religious nature, and most probably the work of prisoners. Many of the historians of the

Castle have quoted the fact that there were vaults within the Keep itself, it can now be stated that during the alterations made to fit the Castle grounds for a pleasure ground, some excavations were specially made to ascertain if this were so, but the result was to entirely negative the suggestion.

GUILDFORD.
(From an old print.)

ABBOT'S HOSPITAL

Is situated on the North side of High Street, opposite Holy Trinity Church. It is a picturesque and well preserved building, and forms one of the most interesting features of the town.

14

It was founded in the seventeenth century by George Abbot, son of an honest clothweaver, and his wife, who resided in Guildford, and whose progeny were both numerous and fortunate. George Abbot, who became Archbishop of Canterbury, was born October 29th, 1562. He was educated at the Free Grammar School, and thence removed to Oxford ; he successively filled the Bishoprics of Lichfield and London, and in 1611 was enthroned in the See of Canterbury.

Abbot was in his high office zealous in carrying out the opinions he embraced in his early life, those of the Calvinists, which rather inclined him to persecution, and occasionally he went beyond the bounds of moderation. The story of the original foundation of the Hospital being brought about by the Archbishop slaying by accident an attendant at the Chase is now discredited, and as a matter of fact was never alluded to by the Archbishop as having taken place. The street front of the building measures eighty-one feet. It has a fine square tower with octagonal turrets. Over the entrance gates is the motto from Virgil "Deus nobis hæc otia fecit." The gates themselves are ornamented with the arms of Abbot and of the Diocese of Canterbury.

Within is a quadrangle of fine proportions. The brothers number twelve and the sisters eight, and they are quartered on either side of the quadrangle.

Several of the rooms are of great interest, and contain carved oak mantel-pieces. In the north-east corner of the building is the chapel, in which are some fine stained glass windows.

The first master of the Hospital was the founder's brother Richard. The Archbishop in addition to founding the Hospital, started a factory for cloth, and a building at the rear was set apart as the manufactory, but this has long since been discontinued. Abbot's monument is at Holy Trinity Church.

Royal Grammar School,

In the upper part of the High Street, was founded by Robert Beckingham, in the reign of Edward VI. Over the entrance are placed the Royal Arms of England, with the inscription, "Scholia Regia Grammaticalis Edwardi Sexti 1550." No less than five prelates of the Church of England received their education here, viz. :—John Parkhurst, Bishop of Norwich, 1560 ; William Cotton, Bishop of Salisbury, 1598 ;

Robert Abbot, Bishop of Salisbury, 1615;
George Abbot, Archbishop of Canterbury, 1610.

St. Mary's Church,

Quarry Street, is a structure the foundation of
which has been attributed to the Testard family,
but is supposed by some to be even older
than their days. The most ancient parts of the
fabric, those beneath and around the tower, are
regarded as Saxon. The church, dedicated to
the Virgin Mary, is built of chalk flints and
pebbles; there are two chapels, one dedicated to
St. John, and the other to St. Mary. These
chapels have circular ends, but it is doubtful if
the chancel was at one time so finished, recent
excavations revealing nothing to prove that
foundations existed in the soil, which is of chalk,
and was evidently undisturbed.

The general architectural characteristics of the
church are Norman, but the styles are mixed, the
nave being separated from the two aisles by
pointed arches. The aisles are broad and the
chancel is raised, doubtless from the configuration
of the ground; it has a richly groined roof. In
the chapel of St. John the Baptist, within the
spandrels of the roof are some curious paintings

executed about the time of Henry III. They are
of a religious character, but it is greatly to be
feared that owing to their situation they will ere
long be lost to view.

THE FRIARY.

There were at one time two monasteries at
Guildford. The principal one, for Black friars,
was situated on the bank of the River Wey,
and in common with other religious houses it
was suppressed in the reign of Henry VIII., and
passed to the Crown.

The old house was pulled down, and the handsome building erected on the site about 1600
was used as the principal lodge to the
Royal Manor. After undergoing a variety of
changes, this house was eventually demolished,
and nothing now remains to indicate that such a
place ever existed, beyond the name of the street.
At the opposite end of the town was a house of
Crutched Friars, known as the Spital of St.
Thomas, this was at the end of Spital Street.

ST. CATHERINE'S CHAPEL

Is in the tything of Artington, in the Parish of
St. Nicholas. It stands on a hill close by the

Portsmouth Road and the River Wey. Tradition speaks of this Chapel and St. Martha's as being built by two sisters. They are, however, situated on what is called "The Pilgrim's Way," and are doubtless in some way connected with that ancient road. St. Catherine's Chapel is mentioned in the pipe rolls of Henry III., and was purchased by Richard de Wauncy, parson of St. Nicholas, 29th Edward I., and by him re-built.

The same Richard also procured a charter for a fair to be held on the hill, and this is still continued every October.

Holy Trinity Church

Stands in the upper part of the High Street; it is a modern structure of red brick. The ancient church was probably built by the Testard family. There were two chantries connected with this church, called Norbrigge and Kingestones. The principal object of interest in the church is the tomb of Archbishop Abbot. The figure of the archbishop is lying at full length on an altar tomb, under a canopy supported by six black marble pillars. The monument was erected at the expense of Sir Maurice Abbot, in 1640. There are other monuments to the memory of Sir Robert Parkhurst, and a brass plate to the memory of the father and mother of the archbishop.

THE CRYPTS.

There are two crypts in the High Street, one under the Angel Hotel, and the other under the premises now occupied by the Savings Bank. It has been stated that these crypts were connected with the castle outworks, but this seems very doubtful, the probability is that at first they were constructed as oratories, and afterwards became storage places for wines, the sale of which was possibly then monopolized by royalty. Between the two crypts originally stood the market cross.

ST. NICHOLAS CHURCH

Is a modern building. Dr. Monsell was one of its former rectors. The Losely Chapel on the south side of the church contains a tomb to a former rector, and the family tomb of the Mores of Losely, near Guildford. Sir Wm. More, and Margaret, his wife, lie buried here, and are represented, the husband in armour, and the wife in the costume of the period.

SUTTON PLACE

Is in the neighbourhood of Guildford, and was built by Sir Richard Weston, in 1523-1525. It is a fine specimen of the architecture of the period, and has been described in minute detail by Mr. Harrison, in his history of the house, published by Messrs. Macmillan. The house is one of the earliest built on the lines of a domestic mansion or manor house, and was evidently a place of "much quietude and retirement." Terra cotta is largely used in its construction, and moulded ornaments are frequent. The designs were evidently those of an Italian artist, who, together with the builder, produced a fine result. The general idea of architecture of the house is Tudor, rather than Gothic, and entirely English in character. The profuse ornamentation is of a very delicate character, and does not follow the rather coarse outlines of the Jacobean and Elizabethan builders.

The use of terra cotta is not unusual in the domestic architecture of this period, as is shown by similar details in the Tower of Layer Marney, in Essex.

A Forgotten Borough.

By George Clinch.

I N many parts of the Weald of Surrey it is only
necessary to take a cross-country walk, away
from the railways, and the beaten track of the
chief roads, in order to discover traces of primitive
manners and speech, and ancient and picturesque
buildings among rural surroundings.

The lower part of the southern slope of the
North Downs is marked by an irregular line of
roadway, upon which are situated many old-
fashioned towns and villages, such as Dorking,
Reigate, Albury, Gomshall, Oxted, Godstone, and
Blechingley. The last named place is of a
peculiarly interesting character. Its wide,
rambling street, its fine church with embattled
tower, and the general style and appearance of
its houses, are all suggestive of ancient importance.
According to popular rumour, Blechingley once
possessed seven churches, and a palace belonging
to Earl Godwin, who is said to have made this
his retreat after his lands in Kent had been

swallowed up by the sea, in the eleventh century. Blechingley Castle, of which only the foundations remained when Bray's account of the parish was written, has also been attributed to Earl Godwin.

It is impossible to say to what extent these vague rumours are founded on truth, but there can be no doubt that Blechingley was a place of importance in early times. At the time of the Domesday Survey, there were two manors here called Civentone and Blachingelie. The first is merely represented by the modern name Chivington, and the latter, by long association, has come to be applied to the whole parish. Nothing definite is known as to the date and builder of the Castle, but at the time of the Domesday Survey it belonged to Richard de Tonbridge, Earl of Clare, and it continued in the possession of the same family for many successive generations. In the year 1263, whilst in the possession of Gilbert de Clare, Earl of Gloucester, it was demolished by the King's forces commanded by Prince Edward, afterwards Edward I. It is understood to have been afterwards restored, and was conveyed by marriage to the Staffords, Dukes of Buckingham. Subsequently it formed a part of the settlement made by Henry VIII. on his divorced queen,

Anne of Cleves. In more recent times it has been owned by the families of Cholmeley and Gaynsford.

Pendell, a fine old mansion in this parish, was built early in the 17th century, and from the discovery of a Roman hypocaust, in an adjoining

BLECHINGLEY.

field, it may be concluded that this district was inhabited at a very early date. During the middle ages, the population probably increased considerably, for, as early as 1294, Blechingley was of sufficient importance to rank as a borough, and to send two members to Parliament.

Previously to 1733, the elections took place in the old-fashioned style in a large house called the Hall, and after that date, at the White Hart Inn. It is recorded that the reversion of the borough upon one occasion was sold for sixty thousand pounds. Anciently the number of electors was about one hundred and thirty, but in more recent times, the voters actually attending the election numbered only about eight or ten. It was one of the most scandalous of all the pocket-boroughs on record, and could scarcely be paralleled except by Gatton and Old Sarum.

The last member for Blechingley was Lord Palmerston, and the borough was disfranchised by the First Reform Act of 1832.

Early Surrey Industries.

By George Clinch.

A MONG many other circumstances which render the county of Surrey remarkable, we must reckon the fact that several of our industries, and the various contrivances for the saving of labour, as well as what may be characterised as luxuries, were introduced into this county at an earlier date than in any other part of the country. The proximity to the British Metropolis may have had something to do with this, but it must also be admitted that the advanced civilization of the inhabitants, and the natural wealth of the soil, have been reasons of a by no means unimportant character.

The manufacture of cloth and woollen goods at Guildford, Godalming, Shere, and the adjacent villages, dates from an early period, and there were in that district some of the earliest paper-mills and fulling-mills in the kingdom.

It is well known that a flourishing trade in iron was carried on in many parts of the Wealden district of Sussex, and in a smaller way, in the Wealds of Surrey and Kent also. The great antiquity to which the industry has been traced back, however, is very remarkable. The Romans extracted iron at Maresfield, Framfield, Sedlescombe, Westfield, and Chiddingly, in Sussex, and probably at Cowden, in Kent. Mr. W. Boyd Dawkins has shown that iron was probably worked near Battle in pre-Roman times.

In the State Paper Office there is still preserved a return, ordered in 1574, of all owners of ironworks in Kent, Surrey, and Sussex. This is the earliest known account which shows the extent to which iron-working in the Weald was carried.

Iron articles made in the Weald are often met with in old farm-houses and cottages. Fire-backs and andirons, or "fire-dogs," and even "tombstones" were frequently made of Weald iron, and at Wadhurst alone there are said to be thirty iron memorials of this kind still remaining.

The cause of the decay of this trade in iron, was not failure of the iron ore, but scarcity of fuel. The serious drain upon the woodlands entailed by charcoal furnaces, led to the passing of acts of parliament for their protection. The act of the first year of Queen Elizabeth did not apply to "the county of Sussex, nor to the Weild of Kent, nor to anie the parishes of Chalewood, Newdigate, and Legh, in the Weild of the countie of Surrey." Another act, passed in the 23rd year of Queen Elizabeth (1581), does not include "the woods of Christopher Darrell, gentleman, in the parish of Newdegate, within the weald of the countie of Surrie, which woods of the said Christopher have heretofore beene, and be by him preserved and coppised for the use of his iron works in those parts." Another act, passed in the 27th year of Queen Elizabeth, and entitled "An act for the preservation of timber in the wilds of the counties of Sussex, Surrey, and Kent, and for the amendment of the high waies, decaied by carriage to and from the iron mils there," prohibits the building of new iron-works, except upon old sites, or where the owner can supply fuel from his own woods.

The final blow to the Wealden iron trade was given by the introduction of pit-coal in smelting. The trade rapidly declined after the year 1735, and in 1828 Ashburnham Furnace, the last in Sussex, was extinguished.

The ore most commonly used was the clay

ironstone, which occurs in nodules and thin beds towards the bottom of what is geologically known as the Wadhurst Clay. It was obtained by means of pits rarely more than twenty feet deep, and widening from a diameter of about six feet at the top to a much greater diameter at the bottom. A great many of the pits remain, and they are generally full of water.

Iron ore in considerable abundance has been found in the south-western part of Surrey, about Haslemere, Dunsfold and Cranley, and in the south-eastern part about Lingfield and Horne. In Surrey and West Sussex, the "ragstone," as it is called, which lies on the Weald Clay, has been used for smelting.

The quaint pages of Aubrey contain the following particulars of a search for coal in the parish of Worplesdon, which are very interesting in view of the recent experimental borings in search of coal in the Wealden area :—

"Mr. Giles Thornborough, Rector of St. Nicholas, and the Holy Trinity, at Guildford, one of His Majesty's chaplains, digging and boring after coal, in Slyfield-green, in this parish, found 1st, of sand and gravel, seven feet depth ; then a spring : within a little of that, a bed of stones like square caps, and about two feet every way; on the outside, whitish; within, full of sulphur, out of which was extracted tin, by Lander Smith, of London, engraver. These stones are called, at the coal-pitts at Newcastle, Catts'-heads, lying always (they say) where coal is. The depth of this bed lay not above one yard. These catts'-heads are all full of small pipes for the mine to breathe through. Next under them, lay a body of black clay (without any stone or mixture) for 15 fathoms; then a rock of stone, about a yard thick, which was very hard; then they came to black clay again for about three fathoms, and then another rock; after that, clay mixed with minerals: then cockle-shells and periwinkle-shells, out of which Prince Rupert extracted tinn and other things, and some filled with clay; after this sprung a bed of oker, 12 foot thick; a kind of mother-of-pearl; after that, a green quicksand. Then came coal, which, how deep it is, is unknown; for here the irons broke, thought by Mr. Lilley, the astrologer, to be by the subterranean spirits; for as fast as the irons were put in they would snap off. This is a kind of rocky coal (like that which they call kennel-coal,) which burns like a candle.

"The inducement to Mr. Thornborough to be at

15

this charge and search, was that there was a kind of stoney coal (that would burn,) which he found by grubbing up the roots of an old oak in his grounds here.

" Fullers'-earth, like clay (which is mixed with brimstone,) lay about 20 fathoms, and one or two yards thick."

The use of regular coal for fuel seems to have been first introduced into the interior part of Surrey at the time the Wey was made navigable from Weybridge to Guildford—towards the end of the 17th century. This means of transit supplied the western part of the county, and in the beginning of the 18th century use was made of the River Wandle for the conveyance of coal as far as Croydon.

In Camden's time there were pits of jet, near Okewood, and Evelyn says that in his time there were " pits of jeate, in the skirts of the parish of Wotton, near Sussex." No traces of jet are now apparent, however.

Fullers' Earth exists in great quantities in the neighbourhood of Nutfield, Blechingley, and Reigate, and it has been dug for commercial purposes for centuries. " The oldest pit now wrought," said a writer in 1813, " is said to have lasted between fifty and sixty years; but it is fast wearing out." . . . "The yellow and blue earths are of different qualities, and are used for different purposes : the former, which is deemed the best, is employed in fulling the kerseymeres and finer cloths of Wiltshire and Gloucestershire ; the blue is principally sent into Yorkshire for the coarser cloths. The price at the pits for either kind is 6s. the ton." In the year 1730 the price of it at the pit was 4d. a sack, and 6s. a load, and in 1744 the price remained nearly the same.

A good many localities in Surrey have yielded brick-earth, and at Nonsuch, in the parish of Cheam, is a very singular and valuable bed of earth, from which bricks capable of resisting an intense heat were made. It was worked at an early date, and from the following account by Leland, it appears to have been used in making crucibles in his time. Speaking of Cuddington (the ancient name of Nonsuch), he says " Crompton, of London, hath a close by Cuddington, in Southery, where the King buildeth. In this close is a vaine of fine yerth, to make moldes for goldsmiths and casters of metale, that a loade of it sold for a crowne of gold. Like yerth is not found in all Englande."

Merstham Stone has been quarried for building purposes for many years. A patent (still in existence) was granted, in the time of Edward III., to one John Thomas Prophete, empowering him to dig Merstham Stone for use at Windsor Castle, and ordering the Sheriff and other officers to aid him by any means in their power. The patent expressly enjoins that such men as refuse to work are to be seized by the Sheriff's officers, and placed in durance vile in the royal castle.

This stone becomes hardened after exposure to the air. The Chapel of Henry VII. at Westminster Abbey was constructed of Merstham Stone.

Firestone is found in considerable quantities in Surrey, and there are quarries of it in the neighbourhood of Godstone, Gatton, Merstham, Reigate, and Blechingley. The stone when first dug out of the quarry, particularly that at Merstham, is soft, and unable to bear the action of a damp atmosphere, but after it has been under cover for a few months, its texture becomes compact, and it will resist the action of fire. There is a variety of this stone found near Blechingley, which was formerly much used by chemists, bakers, and glass-makers. It is much softer than the stone from the other quarries, and requires more skill in working it. Malcolm thus writes of it:—"It is of such a peculiarly fine quality for sustaining the utmost heat, that it is sought after by all the principal glass manufacturers in every part of the kingdom, large quantities being now shipped for Liverpool and the North. It was principally owing to the powerful effects of this stone, which became known to Mr. Dawson, the original proprietor of the Vauxhall plate-glass works, that he was able to produce such amazing plates, as not only to give his glass a decided preference in England, but to astonish even the French themselves, from whom Mr. Dawson discovered the secret of manufacturing plate-glass in the garb of a day-labourer."

Glass-making was once an important Surrey industry, and Chiddingfold has the distinction of being the first recorded place in which the trade was carried on in England. Records have been discovered which prove the supply of glass from Chiddingfold to St. Stephen's Chapel at Westminster in 1350.

Lambeth from the beginning of the seventeenth to the middle of the eighteenth century, possessed an important manufactory of English Delft pottery.   It was, in fact, the most important manufactory of Delft in England, and was introduced by Dutch workmen, who have left on the earlier specimens produced at Lambeth strong marks of Dutch influence.

The chief articles produced were dishes, wine pots inscribed Sack, Whit, and Claret, salt-cellars, and other useful domestic ware.   Among the plates there is a set which often occurs, on which are inscribed the following six doggrel lines :—

1. What is a merry man?
2. Let him do what he can
3. To entertain his guests
4. With wine and merry jests.
5. But if his wife do frown
6. All merriment goes down.

The manufacture of gunpowder was carried on at a very early date in Surrey.   About the year 1590, George Evelyn, grandfather of the diarist, received the royal licence to erect powder mills at Long Ditton and Godstone.   The art of making gunpowder is said to have been brought from Holland by the Evelyn family.   In 1626 the East India Company's powder-works were in existence in Surrey.

The first mills in England for casting, hammering, and wiring brass, were erected at Wotton in

Surrey. The mode in which the operations were performed shows the rude state of knowledge and machinery at that time. "First," says Evelyn in a letter to Aubrey, "they drew the wire by men sitting harnessed in certain swings, taking hold of the brass thongs fitted to the holes, with pincers fastened to a girdle which went about them, and then with stretching forth their feet against a stump, they shot their bodies from it, closing with the plate again; but afterwards this was quite left off, and the effect performed by an *ingenio* brought out of Sweden."

The first brass-works in England are said to have been put into operation, in 1649, at Esher, in Surrey, where rosette-copper, imported from Sweden, was exclusively employed in the manufacture; the proprietor having, however, become involved in a disastrous law-suit, the establishment was ultimately broken up.

These works are said to have been established by some German adventurers.

The first clover grown in England, was grown in Surrey, having been introduced from Flanders, in 1645, by Sir Richard Weston, of Sutton, near Guildford. Sir Richard also introduced into Surrey from the Netherlands the contrivances for

the improvement of river navigation, known as
locks.   This was between 1645 and 1650, and the
locks on the Wey, between Guildford and
Weybridge, which were formed under his
direction, are supposed to be some of the first of
their kind, if not actually the first erected in the
kingdom.   It was not until about the end of the
17th century, however, that the system of
navigation was completed.   In the year 1760, the
navigation was extended as far as Godalming,
four locks being constructed between that place
and Guildford.   A writer, in 1813, mentions that
there were then ten barges of forty-five tons
belonging to the inhabitants of Godalming.

Sir Francis Carew, who married the niece of
Sir Walter Raleigh, is said to have planted
orange seeds, which produced some orange trees,
at Beddington.   Bishop Gibson, in his additions
to Camden's *Britannia*, speaks of them as having
been there for a hundred years previous to 1695.
As these trees produced fruit, they could not have
been raised from seeds; but they may have been
brought from Portugal, or from Italy, as early as
the close of the 16th century.

The trees at Beddington were planted in the
open ground, with a movable cover to screen

them from the severe weather of winter. They had attained the height of eighteen feet, and the stems were about nine inches in diameter, in the beginning of the eighteenth century; while the spread of the head of the largest one was twelve feet one way, and nine the other. There had always been a wall on the north side of them, to screen them from the cold of that quarter, but they were at such a distance from the wall as to have room to spread, and plenty of air and light. In 1738 they were surrounded by a permanent inclosure, like a greenhouse. They were all destroyed in the following winter; but whether owing to the severe frost, or partly to the confinement and damp of the permanent enclosure, cannot now be ascertained.

Sir Francis Carew appears to have been very skilful in the culture of fruit trees. It was he who caused a cherry-tree to be enclosed by a damp canvas cover, whereby the ripening of the fruit was delayed till the expected visit of Queen Elizabeth occurred. This was quite a month after the season for cherries was over in England.

Mortlake was once celebrated for the manufacture of fine tapestry, an industry which was established in 1619 by Sir Francis Crane, Knt., under the patronage of James I. Charles I. also encouraged the art by liberal grants of money. In 1623 the celebrated Francis Cheyne, a native of Bostock, in Lower Saxony, was engaged as limner. Many beautiful designs were wrought, including subjects in history and grotesque.

The tapestry works fell into complete disuse after they were deprived of the royal patronage in the time of Charles II.

One of the first iron railways for horse power constructed in the kingdom, and what may be looked upon as the immediate precursor of the steam railways which were destined to revolutionize the whole region near London a few years later, was that between Wandsworth and Merstham, which was projected and begun in 1802 and 1803. The part which extended from Wandsworth to Croydon was soon completed, and it proved so successful as to induce the proprietors to carry it on to Merstham.

For the purpose of forming a junction between the Thames and the railway, a large basin was constructed at Wandsworth, capable of holding more than thirty barges. The line was double, and as far as possible followed the ground, which was naturally level. It was also so planned as to

approach as near as might be to the numerous
manufactories, which at that time covered the
banks of the Wandle. Short branch lines
connected such as lay out of the course of the
main line of railway, and a contemporary account
informs us, " In order that the waggon going in
one direction may return at any part of the route,
there are at short distances diagonal railways
and a bar of iron moving on a pivot : by turning
this bar the waggon can be moved from one line
to the other." Thus were our notions about
"points" anticipated.

Great surprise was manifested at the ease with
which great weights could be pulled along by
horse power, and in order to demonstrate how
useful the system of iron-rails was likely to become,
a "bet was made between two gentlemen, that a
common horse could draw thirty-six tons for six
miles along the road, and that he should draw
this weight from a dead pull, as well as turn it
round the occasional windings of the road. The
24th of July, 1805, was fixed on for the trial,
when a number of gentlemen assembled near
Merstham, to see this extraordinary triumph of
art. Twelve waggons loaded with stones, each
waggon weighing above three tons, were chained

together, and a horse, taken promiscuously from the timber-cart of Mr. Harwood, was yoked into the team. He started from near the Fox public-house, and drew the immense chain of waggons with apparent ease to near the turnpike at Croydon, a distance of six miles, in one hour and forty-one minutes, which is nearly at the rate of four miles an hour. In the course of this time he stopped four times, to show that it was not by the impetus of the descent that the power was acquired; and after each stoppage he drew off the chain of waggons from a dead rest. Having gained his wager, Mr. Banks ordered four more loaded waggons to be added to the cavalcade, with which the same horse again set off with undiminished power; and still further to show the effect of the railway in facilitating motion, he directed the attending workmen, to the number of about fifty, to mount on the waggons, when the horse proceeded without the least distress. After the trials the waggons were taken to the weighing machine; and it appeared that the total weight was above fifty-five tons."

It was of course necessary that the railway should be as nearly level as possible, and from the earliest times it was foreseen that the chief cost of constructing them would arise from the expense attending the levelling of the ground, in places which were not naturally even. In constructing this railway from Wandsworth to Croydon, there was little difficulty or trouble, but in extending it to Merstham there were many difficulties, and much expense was incurred. Several valleys from ten to thirty feet deep lay in the way, which it was necessary to fill up, and some arches had to be thrown across other parts of the road. A little beyond the Red Lion at Smitham Bottom, an embankment twenty feet high was thrown up, and an archway had to be constructed in it sufficiently high to admit the passage underneath of a waggon loaded with hay, straw, or other materials from the Downs and Caterham Valley to the London Road. In another part of this railway it was found necessary to hollow out the ground, where an arch was constructed, so that sufficient height of arch was obtained without raising the level of the railway too much.

In these days when the whole areas around London and other large towns are so thickly populated, it seems strange to look back no farther than the beginning of this century, when a solitary railroad for horse-power penetrated into the wild region as far only as Merstham. A contemporary writer upon the subject says :—" Notwithstanding the advantages of iron railways with respect to facility and motion, this road does not appear to be much used, nor is it probable that railways will ever come into general use. The expense attending the formation of them, except where the ground is naturally level, is enormous; and it is evident that the advantages, and consequently the gain, are confined to carriage in one direction. The iron railway from Croydon to Wandsworth lies in the neighbourhood of so many extensive manufactures, that it may possibly answer; but the division from Merstham to Croydon, running through a tract of country destitute of manufactures, and having only the limes, fuller's-earth, stone, and corn to depend upon at the further extremity, can never pay very well."

Bygone Merton.

BY REV. E. A. KEMPSON, M.A.

THE once famous Merton Abbey is gone, and the gallant Lord Nelson has passed away, but happily the very ancient church is not gone, nor the quaint old church house opposite—and the river Wandle is still the boundary on the Mitcham side : water suffers less change than land, as Tennyson says :—

> " For men may come, and men may go,
> But I flow on for ever."

Only in the present day anything worthy of the name of a river must be useful as a condition of its existence, and during its short course from the Banstead hills, there are few rivers in the country which turn so many mills, and supply so many fish-ponds, as the river Wandle. One of the pastimes of Lord Nelson in his later years (which he spent at Merton), was to divert some of the waters of the Wandle through his small domain, and call it the "Nile," but this has been filled up long ago, and houses built upon the site.

An old man named Hudson, who died a few years ago, at the age of ninety-five, used to state that, as a boy, he often saw Nelson fishing in the Wandle, near the Abbey Mill—that he would often stop and speak kindly to the boys in the street, who regarded his weather-beaten form and features possibly with all the more reverence because of the fruit and pence which he used to bestow upon the youngsters. This old man boasted that he had the honour of shutting the door of the post chaise, in which, early on the morning of September 13th, 1805, the gallant admiral, so soon afterwards doomed to fall at Trafalgar, drove off from the gates of Merton Place. This house at first really belonged to Sir William and Lady Hamilton, but afterwards it appears to have been bought by Nelson, who left the property as a legacy to Lady Hamilton.

Of Merton Abbey, when it was in its glory, little is known. No engraving of it is known to exist. Nor is there even a plan of the sixty acres on which it stood, surrounded by a wall of flint, stone, and Roman bricks, which, for a few yards, is the only reminder left by the ruthless hand of the spoiler.

The original Abbey was a wooden building,

erected in 1115, by Gilbert Norman, near the Parish Church, which he is also said to have built at about the same date. Here he founded a Convent of Augustinian Canons, an institution which in after years became famous as a home of learning and piety. It was granted by the founder to Robert Bayle, a sub-prior of Austin Canons. Two years later the establishment was moved to a second house, whither the prior and his fifteen brethren went in procession singing the hymn, " Salve dies."

In 1121, Henry I. granted the entire manor of Merton to the canons in return for £100 in silver, and six marks of gold. Then the first stone priory was built, the foundation stone being laid with great solemnity by Gilbert Norman, who died the same year.

In 1236, was held here the great council of the nation, which passed the well-known Statutes of Merton, remarkable for their Protestant character. The king and the pope endeavoured to put England under canon law, which would have been the death blow to all her greatness. But they were steadily confronted by the Barons, who made the famous declaration, " We are unwilling that the laws of England should be changed,"

16

re-echoed later on in the thirty-nine articles, " The Pope of Rome hath no jurisdiction in this realm of England."

This was one of the mitred abbeys which sent a representative to parliament, and was the nurse of several great men, including Thomas à Beckett and Walter de Merton, who was at the same time Lord Chancellor of England, and Bishop of Rochester. His tomb may be seen in the Cathedral. He died in October 1277. In the Bodleian Library, at Oxford, there are the Chronicles of Merton Abbey, which contain the ordinances of William de Wykeham for its government. The canons were forbidden to hunt, or to keep dogs for that purpose, on penalty of being confined to a diet of bread and ale during six holidays. It appears, however, that the canons were not as obedient as they ought to have been, and were censured by the Bishop of Winchester at one of his visitations for not attending Mass, and for carrying bows and arrows.

Nearly all the Plantagenet and Lancastrian Kings granted charters to the abbey, and it became very rich, with a rent roll of £1000 a year, besides advowsons of many churches in Surrey and other counties.

Henry VIII., as was his wont, quietly suppressed the abbey, and coolly appropriated its revenues. Its buildings became a garrison, and orders were given "to make Farnham Castle indefensible, and secure Merton Abbey and other places of strength in the same county." Queen Elizabeth leased the buildings with the Merton lands to Sir Gregory Lovell, her treasurer, for twenty-one years, at an annual rent of £26 13s. 4d., and paid him in 1571 a visit of three days. He built a mansion after the style of the period, which still exists, working up into it the materials of the dismantled abbey. And now the remorseless railway between Wimbledon and Tooting runs through the property—leaving the house on one side, and the interesting old Norman archway by which it was approached, on the other.

In 1724 and 1752 two calico printing works were established within the walls, and a copper mill erected, which, in the year 1790, employed 1000 persons.

These manufactories have been in turn superseded by the silk printing works of Messrs. Littler, and the artistic fabrics and glass painting works of Mr. Morris—" A pleasing contrast," one chronicler observes, " to the monastic indolence which reigned here in the gloomy ages of superstition."

The Parish Church, dedicated to the Virgin Mary, is probably one of the most curious in the neighbourhood of London—the nave and chancel are of almost equal length—and the latter has an almost unique decorated roof of chestnut wood.

The north door opens under a Norman arch with zigzag mouldings, and the hammered iron work of the original oaken door is of a remarkably interesting character. A church is recorded to have existed here in the Doomsday Book, and with the exception of the side aisles, which are later additions done in very good taste, the present structure is probably that built by Gilbert Norman, the founder of the abbey.

There belongs to the church a large picture of the descent from the Cross. It is much damaged, but appears to have been a good painting, and was either the work of Luca Jordano or a copy from him.

On the walls of the nave still hang several hatchments belonging to great families once connected with the parish. Among them is that of Lord Nelson, whose church seat is still shown in the vestry.

Opposite the church is an Elizabethan mansion, known as church house. It stands in a garden of at least two acres, and is surrounded by walls quite as massive as those of the old abbey. It has had a chequered history. At the end of last century it was for a time the residence of Richard Brinsley Sheridan, and was doubtless often visited by the great Dr. Johnson. Soon afterwards it was used as a convalescent hospital in connection with Bermondsey workhouse; but the black plague cleared off most of the inmates, and the rest fled in terror, so that it was left desolate for a time. The iron entrance gate opposite the Church is very fine, and at the other side of the house there was a similar entrance, now blocked up, leading by a noble avenue of elms to the London and Kingston Road.

Index.

250   *INDEX.*

Macaulay, Lord, 176, 180, 181
Macaulay, Zachary, 179, 181
Macintosh, Sir James, 184
Mandeville, Sir G. de, 164, 165
Manningham, Sir Richard, 104
Marlowe, Christopher, 132
Marshalsea, The, 136
Massinger Phillip, 132, 133
Mary of Scotland, 122
Mermaid Club, 131
Merstham, 228, 234, 235, 237, 238
Merton, Walter de, 242
Merton, Statutes of, 241, 242
Merton Abbey, 239, 243
Merton Church, 244, 245
Merton, Church House, 245
Milton Street, 92
Mitcham, 239
Moncton Hook, 85
Moor Park, 105
Morden, 84
More, Sir Thomas, 21, 29
More, Sir William, 193, 194, 215
Mortlake, 233
Morton, Cardinal, 10, 23, 36, 39
Morton's Tower, Lambeth Palace, 24
Mowbray, Dr., 104

Nag's Head Conspiracy, 36-37
Nelson, Lord, 259, 245
Netley Heath, 90
Newdigate, 189, 223
Newlands, Abraham, 136
Nonsuch Palace, 186-203, 227
Norbury, 150
Norman, Gilbert, 241, 244
Norwood, 141, 155, 158
Nower, The, 93
Nunciata, Toto dell, 187
Nutfield, 226
Nycolson, James, 127

Oakwood Hill, 85
Oatlands, 199
Ockley, 83, 85
Odin, 98
Okewood, 226
Oursiau, Nicholas, 191
Oxted, 217

Palmerston, Lord, 220
Paris Gardens, 135

Parish, Rev. W. D., 43
Park Hatch, 92
Parker, Archbishop, 36, 37, 143, 145, 195
Peckham, Archbishop, 29
Pegge, Dr., 43
Penselwood, 95
Peperharrow, 7
Perrot, Alan, 120
Pickle Herring Stairs, 120
Pilgrim's Way, 4, 87-94
Pitt, William, 178, 179
Plaistow, Sussex, 85
Pole, Cardinal, 193
Pollock, Sir George, 184
Pont de l'Arche, William, 123, 124
Pope, Sir Thomas, 121
Popham, Sir John, 133
Prophete, J. T., 228
Puttenham, 8, 9
Puttenham Common, 204
Puttenham Priory, 90

Raleigh, Sir Walter, 131, 196, 232
Reigate, 189, 217, 226, 228
Reynolds, Archbishop, 25
Richmond, 199
Robert of Paris, 135
Roches, Peter des, 124, 127
Rome Farm, 85
Rowhook, 83, 84, 85
Rudgwick, 84

Sacheverell, Dr., 136
St. André, Mr. 104
St. Catherine's Hill, 90, 99
St. George's Hill, 93, 94
St. John, Walter, 171
St. Magnus' Church, 116
St. Martha's Hill, 90, 99, 112
St. Mary Overie, 115, 119, 121, 124, 125
St. Olave's Church, 116
St. Saviour's Church, 115
St. Saviour's Dock, 121
St. Saviour's School, 136
St. Swithin, 116
Sancroft, Archbishop, 30, 38
Sandal Lane, 92
Sandall, Bishop, 134
Sanderstead, 96
Scarbrook, 152
Scory, Bishop, 143
Seale, 8